JOAN DIDION

JOAN DIDION
THE LAST INTERVIEW
and OTHER CONVERSATIONS

with an introduction by PATRICIA LOCKWOOD

MELVILLE HOUSE
BROOKLYN • LONDON

CONTENTS

INTRODUCTION

PATRICIA LOCKWOOD

The first thoughts about Joan Didion are not reasonable. The present literature about her is a hagiography that does not entirely trust itself; there is a vacancy at the center of it that I call the "but surely." But surely if these essays were published now, the hagiography says to itself at three in the morning, they would meet with a different reception? But surely if she wrote today, her ideas about feminism would be more in line with ours? But surely, for all her pointillism, she is failing to draw the conclusions we would most like to see? The hagiography turns the pillow over, looking for a cool spot. How much can we really rely on someone who loved the Doors? Why do all her last lines give the impression that she's speaking from beyond the veil? What, in the end, is she actually saying? But surely she has told us that herself, and all along. What she is saying, standing in the corner of every piece, holding her yellow legal pad and watching, is: "I was there."

In a 2017 documentary directed by her nephew Griffin Dunne, this three-in-the-morning question is absent. It begins with a bridge and a blur, close-ups of bare feet and fresh typewriter ink. A rat crawls over a hippie, to show that in the Swinging Sixties, anything can happen. When Didion herself appears, her mouth is bright with lipstick and amused. Her gestures are as large as fireworks. She puts her whole self into the process of speaking, moving her hands as if she's flinging handfuls of certainty away from her body. Charcoal cashmere and a slender chain; her hair the correct camel of a good coat. In a scene where she reads her own writing, she looks happy, and tastes one or two words longer than the others, for their well-chosenness. It calls to mind Maria Wyeth in *Play It as It Lays*, distinguishing between "the right bracelet and the amusing impersonation of the right bracelet and the bracelet that was merely a witless copy."

Still, there are oversized clues to the fact that the subject is out of the ordinary. At one point Dunne asks her how it felt to see the five-year-old child on acid when she was reporting in Haight-Ashbury. Her face works, and you are expecting her to say: "It was horrifying." Instead a light breaks, and she says: "It was gold."

I thought of her essay about John Wayne—Didion loved him, and not just because he gathered the whole American West in a man. It was also because, as Katharine Hepburn

observed, it was so thrilling to lean against him. Great like
a tree, a place to rest. And didn't she want to rest? Weren't
her burdens so heavy? In youth she had rested against the
strength, the solid thereness of the West; in adulthood, didn't
she become paralyzed when she felt it could no longer hold
her? When she headed to San Francisco in 1967, wasn't it
because she suddenly saw America as a power that could no
longer shoulder its people?

Order, she sought order. "I have a very rigid sense of
right and wrong," she told Sara Davidson in 1977. "Behavior
is right or wrong. I was once having dinner with a psychiatrist
who told me that I had monocular vision, and there was no
need for everything to be right or wrong. Well, that way lies
madness."

There is no new information here, because we have had
it already from Didion herself. We know she was born in
1934, and we see the disturbed and settled dust of the Sacramento Valley where she was raised, and we hear the family
conversations about land changing hands. Her father, Frank
Reese, an army air corps officer, was dogged by depression to
the point of hospitalization. Her mother, Eduene, last in a
long line, stamped with all the attributes we might expect a
woman named Eduene to have, and provider of the particular
totems her daughter would come to assign weight to in her
turn. We are familiar with the "insistently ironic" first story
Didion wrote at the age of five, in which a freezing woman
wakes to find she is actually dying of heat at the edge of the
desert. We know about the seven years at *Vogue*, after Berkeley, where she learned to choose the right word; we know
about the forty-year marriage to John Gregory Dunne, who

was "between me and the world"—though it is surprising to hear her speak in Dunne's documentary of how it happened: "Well I went to Hartford, and fell in love with his family, and determined that I was going to marry him. And did." Here her face becomes heavy with the curse of heterosexuality. "I don't know what fall in love means. It's not part of my world. But I do remember having a very clear sense that I wanted this to continue. I liked being a couple. I liked having somebody there. It could not have been somebody who wasn't a writer. Only because that person would not have had any patience with me."

Coca-Colas in the morning. Yellow Corvettes and Vanda orchids, the shuffle of the surf in Malibu and the view from the window of the Royal Hawaiian Hotel. There are the beads on her newly born daughter's wrist that spell N. I. for "No Information"; there is the territory on the map for which they named her, Quintana Roo. There is John baptizing Quintana in the sink the night they adopted her so that she might not, God forbid, go to limbo. There he is at the dinner table with his left hand raised, slumped motionless and Didion saying, automatically, "Don't do that"—and there is Quintana at 39 in the ICU, dying of acute pancreatitis. We can even, if you're still with us, travel all the way back and tell you how Didion is descended from people who "parted ways" with the Donners out West, which means the story she was raised with was one that showed how it could all go to hell in an instant, how unexpectedly a party could turn into people eating each other. We know enough for her to become a background against which we try to make sense of the rest.

"I have figured out her rhythm," I once told a friend in a diner in Iowa City, though I will not tell you what I ate, or what I was wearing. (A hamburger? Some sort of shirt?) "Her sentences are smooth, are smooth, are smooth, and then three-quarters of the way through the landing gear drops down." Her syntax returns to itself at the end, because it belongs to the structures of Henry James. This, combined with a straightforwardness of diction from Hemingway, gives you the sensation that you are going somewhere, then landing. And all the while you're flying, music is piped in, poetry, a high-toned jingle in the collective head.

I recalled that as I read *South and West*, which must hold a curious place in Didion's oeuvre as the book she could not write. The second section is comprised of notes she took during the Patty Hearst trial, which eventually led to a broader book about California called *Where I Was From*. (I prefer these notes to that book; they exhibit a murderous compression.) The first section, and the majority, is comprised of notes she made during a month she spent in the South with her husband in 1970; at the beginning, she explains that, "at the time, I had thought it might be a piece."

It was not. The elements are there: around the hotel swimming pools, the Confederate flag towels contrast with her own cosmopolitan bikini. She writes of trains, highways, snakes, kudzu—networks and infrastructure, which she understands and on which she relies, versus biology, overgrowth and festering, which threaten to suck her in and incorporate her. She interviews the white owner of a "black radio station." The dialogues of strangers shed their usual light. When it's

xii   Introduction

all too much, she escapes to the cool air-conditioning of the mall. Her husband drives but is not there. He is not much mentioned, except when she says "we."

At the center of this story there is a terrible secret, a kernel of cyanide, and the secret is that the story doesn't matter, doesn't make any difference, doesn't figure. The snow still falls in the Sierra. The Pacific still trembles in its bowl. The great tectonic plates strain against each other while we sleep and wake. Rattlers in the dry grass. Sharks beneath the Golden Gate. In the South they are convinced that they have bloodied their place with history. In the West we do not believe that anything we do can bloody the land, or change it, or touch it.

They are convinced, but we believe. The West is the sunset all heroes walk towards. But she understands by instinct that if the South is interrogated too far, too deeply, then all the myths we tell ourselves about America collapse.

It is a slim entry in her canon, but for the first time in a long while, I felt as if someone was on track. She was right that the South was both a begetting stain and an arrow to the future; the future it pointed to is here. She was right that it was the "secret source," the "psychic center." It must have been that powerful, or Americans would not today be living in its mind—among those "secret frontiersmen who walk around right in the ganglia of the fantastic electronic pulsing that is life in the United States and continue to receive information only through the most tenuous chains of rumor, hearsay, haphazard trickledown" she invoked in "Notes towards a Dreampolitik."

To revisit *Slouching towards Bethlehem* and *The White Album* is to read an old up-to-the-minute relevance renewed. Inside these essays, the coming revolution feels neither terrifying nor exhilarating but familiar—if you are a reader of Joan Didion, you have been studying it all your life. Read "Comrade Laski, C.P.U.S.A. (M.-L.)" and see if you do not recognize the man in the modern scene. "Actually I was interested not in the revolution but in the revolutionary." Where things are moving too fast she fixes a focal point. She captures the way the language becomes more memetic, more meaningless just as the ground begins to swell under the feet—as if the herd, sensing some danger, must consolidate its responses. Her adept turn to political writing in the 1980s and 1990s showed the same prescience; if you are tuned to where the language goes strange, you will anticipate the narrative they're going to try to sell you.

She herself is now powerful, runs the criticism. There is a danger in her, and it is the same danger she suggests in "Some Dreamers of the Golden Dream": that the stories first tell us what it was like, and then they tell us how to live. Like the desert, she imposes a style. "Our favorite people and our favorite stories become so not by any inherent virtue, but because they illustrate something deep in the grain, something unadmitted."

There is something to this. Her essays take place, for many people, in some innermost hotel room. We are there as she unpacks the items on her iconic list, sets the bottle of bourbon on the desk, calls home to check the time, lies down in the dark when the aura comes. Why are we closer to her? Why do we feel, along with her, the shaking of the hand narrowing down and down to the steadiness of the pen? A peculiarity of my own: among all her books, I had not read *The Year of Magical Thinking*, because my own husband, whom I married very young, on whom I depend and in whom I store half of my information, has a family history of heart attacks—to be more specific, the men on his father's side all drop dead in their homes at the age of 59. "As long as I don't read it," I often thought to myself, and thought no further, though I kept the book on a low shelf. Whenever the swimming-pool color of the spine caught my eye I saw a kitchen, and a telephone on the wall with a long curling cord, and my own hands not knowing what to do. "As long as I save it, against that day."

This is personal, but we have seen both the deep personal and the wide diagnostic in her, it is all tied together: South and West, the fracturing 1960s, a line of ancestry across the country. The earth rucking up like a dress bought where, bought when. The wagon train and the plane rides of the sentences. Someone's on track. The assay scales and the choosing of the words. Her grandfather a geologist, herself a seismograph, her daughter sobbing "Let me be in the ground." The cowboy and the one who strides beside him, the Broken Man, the childhood bogeyman Quintana and she so feared. These things are together in our reading. Through long investigation into fracture she has brought them together, and somehow we are there in the center of her thinking, in the place where she is working it all out. We are told it does not hold. It holds.

Perhaps she promises that synthesis, even of a time like this, is still possible. "Something happened—the ease of my relationship with language disappeared . . . Ease in producing words. But they did mean something." Perhaps she offers the feeling that if you write the facts down, the facts might somehow remain standing at the end, after the end. There is a small, unobtrusive reporter in the corner. She has outlasted everything else.

Other observations are there. She sounds, at times, as if a huge crow is about to land on her right shoulder. She breathes the Santa Ana instead of the air. It would be possible to write a parody of her novels called *Desert Abortion—in a Car.* Possible, but why? The best joke you could make wouldn't touch her. Not the solidity of what she has done, which can be leaned against like John Wayne. Which, for all the claims of its paranoia, dislocation, fragility offers what none of her critics would ever suspect: an assurance of thereness, of hereness, of that good strong frame. Rest.

JOAN DIDION

THE FEMALE ANGST

INTERVIEW BY SALLY DAVIS
PACIFICA RADIO
FEBRUARY 10, 1972

SALLY DAVIS: Joan Didion has written, in addition to a vast body of nonfiction for *The Saturday Evening Post* and other American magazines, two novels, and has published a collection of her best nonfiction pieces, *Slouching Towards Bethlehem*. She writes of the confusion and awfulness of modern life; of death by violence, murder, rattlesnake bites, terrible acts of God, evil winds, and the inability of things to hold at the center; the universal falling apart. She has been called this generation's supreme chronicler of angst, she has the ability to show us her own personal pain and in so doing mirror—in the way that Anaïs Nin was talking about earlier—the savagery of nature while shielding us from it. This is a piece from *Play It as It Lays*:

> In January there were poinsettias in front of all the bungalows between Melrose and Sunset, and the rain set in, and Maria wore not sandals but real shoes and a Shetland sweater she had bought in New York the year she was nineteen. For days during the rain she did not speak out loud or read a newspaper. She could not read newspapers because certain stories leapt at her from the page: the four-year-olds in the abandoned refrigerator, the tea party with

Purex, the infant in the driveway, rattlesnake in the playpen, the peril, unspeakable peril, in the everyday. She grew faint as the processions swept before her, the children alive when last scolded, dead when next seen, the children in the locked car burning, the little faces, helpless screams. The mothers were always reported to be under sedation. In the whole world there was not as much sedation as there was instantaneous peril.

Joan, the *National Review*, in one of their reviews of . . . I think it was *Slouching Towards Bethlehem* . . . said of you: "She's passed beyond optimism and pessimism to a far country of quiet anguish, bringing the scant comfort." I wonder what the sources of that anguish are chiefly, and how much of it has to do with being a woman.

JOAN DIDION: Oh, I don't think any of it does, and I don't know—I don't think of myself as an anguished person particularly. But I'm not optimistic and I'm not pessimistic. The way I think doesn't seem to me to have a great deal specifically to do with being a woman. I wasn't brought up too terribly aware of any kind of special woman's role. I mean, it just never occurred to me that anything would be expected of me other than doing whatever I wanted to do. And I don't feel very specifically aware of women's anguish as opposed to general anguish, to the anguish of being a human being.

DAVIS: Well, I know that you write about the anguish, for instance, of war and the anguish of the human condition as manifested in things like Haight-Ashbury and the drug culture and so on—but very often your metaphors, if you like, for the general angst that goes on in you are female ones. For instance, you're talking about, at one point in *Slouching Towards Bethlehem*, going over the edge into some kind of loss of control, some kind of madness, which shows itself with the sardine tins in the sink and the general slovenliness of the house, which is a kind of a very female concept.

DIDION: Well, that comes up because, you know, I am a woman and so I do think the images that come to a woman's mind tend to be female, I suppose, and I write women with more facility than I write men, and that's how that happens. But I don't—I did write a man once that I liked, I mean I wrote a man once in my first novel, who I was as close to as the woman in that novel, although the woman was the main character, and I thought that he came off as well as the woman, but it was the only time I've ever really gotten into a man's—

DAVIS: Psyche.

DIDION: Yeah.

DAVIS: Maria, in *Play It as It Lays,* is almost the story of a kind of chronicle of anguish and fear, which strikes me as being—her anguish is particularly female, particularly concerning her daughter and the feelings about her daughter and her abortion and all of those images; all of the manifestations of her fear are particularly female ones.

DIDION: Well, one of the things I was interested in in that book, I mean one of the things that started coming out of it as I was writing it, was the kind of chain of—I mean this isn't what the book was about, but one of the things that kept coming was that kind of chain between generations of women, between Maria and her daughter, and when she was particularly concerned about her daughter and about aborting the child, I found her thinking naturally about her mother. I mean, it seemed to me to be some kind of chain of things understood by women that comes down, but that I don't know what that means.

DAVIS: She's a particularly California kind of type. Her problems are particularly California ones and her way of coping with them like, you know, working out how she's going to negotiate the freeways every day and so on. And I wondered about, if you feel particularly sensitive towards the pains and the difficulties of living, why you would choose to live your life in California where those difficulties seem to be immensely intensified.

DIDION: Well, I was born in California and lived in New York for eight years, and then after I was married, we moved to Los Angeles, which is a very different place from the place where I come from. And, well, I could only talk about it in two ways. One is that I find it easier to live here, I mean easier in physical terms. I like living here. The other is, that if there is, if there is a place that is—if there is a place in the world that seems to me more real than any other place, I would rather be living there. California in many ways, or Los

Angeles in many ways, strikes me as a very—I feel very close to the reality of something here, where I ceased feeling that way in New York.

DAVIS: What kind of reality are you talking about?

DIDION: What Maria's going through in that book is that she's coming to terms with the meaninglessness of experience, and that's what everybody who lives in Los Angeles essentially has to come to terms with because none of it seems to mean anything.

DAVIS: Is it kind of confronting the worst that there is and then being able to cope with anything else that comes along?

DIDION: Yeah, I would think that is what people ought to do—yeah.

DAVIS: Because Dory Previn, of course, who is also on this program, feels pretty much the way you do that—I mean for her reality is even more important because the grasp on reality is harder for her to maintain, and she maintains that this is the only place that she can feel it.

DIDION: Feel it, yeah. I would find it very difficult to live in a sheltered way because I would keep feeling that I was missing the point.

DAVIS: As you said, you're not optimistic, and you're not pessimistic, but you obviously have enough sensitivity to grasp that life is essentially, as you say, meaningless, if you like. Do you then seek out subjects to intensify this, to show this meaninglessness? I mean, for instance, things like—I understood you were going to work on a book on Linda Kasabian, and you'd written a long piece on Haight-Ashbury and the Lucille Miller case, and all of the most painful things you could get your hands on, really.

DIDION: I'm not doing the book on Linda Kasabian now. I was working on one for a while. Well, there's certain things— I mean it's not consciously seeking things out, but there's certain things that engage your imagination or don't, and sometimes something just sounds exactly . . .

DAVIS: What you're looking for?

DIDION: What you want, well, not what you want, but what— this is something you have to do and I guess in that way it's an unconscious seeking out of . . .

DAVIS: Your piece on the Haight was really—the thousands and thousands and probably millions of words that were written about that situation, yours seemed to me to get to the heart of it more than anything else, and yet you said that you felt—I think you said frustrated—after it was published. That you were unhappy about it.

DIDION: Well, it was a very odd piece to do because I was there for quite a long time, longer than I'd ever spent before on a piece or after, and I kept staying because I kept having the sense that I wasn't getting it. I did not understand what was going on, and I finally came home, and I still didn't think I had it. I mean I still, you know, sometimes . . . Usually on a piece, there comes a day when you know you never have to do another interview. You can go home, you've gotten it. Well that day never came on that piece. The piece had to be written right away. So I wrote it right away. But I wrote it just in a series of scenes, exactly how it happened to me, and that was the only way that I could write it because I had no conclusions at all.

DAVIS: But at the end of it did you still feel that you hadn't, even though it was highly praised and other people obviously thought that you had said something significant about the whole movement?

DIDION: That piece is a blank for me still. I have no idea whether it was good or bad.

DAVIS: You zeroed in—as I notice you often do in other pieces—on the children as being—I mean I think there was three-year-old Michael, who lived in this kind of appalling barn thing and started a fire, and the little girl, Susan, who was on acid at five. Is that part of your being a mother, do you think?

DIDION: Well, that was very real to me then because I had a two-year-old at the time that I was working on that, and so it was particularly vivid to me to see these other children, and it was particularly vivid to me because I was away from the two-year-old and feeling slightly . . .

DAVIS: Cut off?

DIDION: Cut off from her, yeah.

DAVIS: How much of your time, how much of your fears of living (if that's the expression) kind of zero in on Quintana, your own child?

DIDION: Well not a great deal. She's very—I mean I am apprehensive about everything and anxious, so I have to try to not lay this on her, and anyways she wouldn't have any of it if I did try.

DAVIS: You described her at one point as being the kind of child that likes to get up in the morning.

DIDION: Oh yeah, she's very competent.

DAVIS: Which brings me back to your own childhood and the piece you wrote in *Slouching Towards Bethlehem* about keeping a notebook. The way you told what to me seemed an incredible story about your mother giving you this notebook, and the first story you chose to note down in that was about the woman who thought she was freezing to death in Alaska or something and woke up to find that she was dying of heat in the Sahara. I think you were five, you said.

DIDION: Yeah.

DAVIS: And I wondered what kind of sensibility in a child can possibly take that kind of a story and put it down as the first entry in her new notebook.

DIDION: Well, you know, I read someplace once that children, people in the nursery, within hours after birth, some children you can poke, the doctor can poke them and they don't flinch, and some children flinch. And then they've done studies about these children, and the children who flinch turn out to be flinchers all their life, and the others are extroverted or happy or competent children like my daughter. I think I was just a flincher at birth.

DAVIS: You're not a subscriber to environment, obviously, because your own environment sounded very stable.

DIDION: Well, it was, it was very stable. My brother is an entirely different kind of person from me. It was mystifying to my mother and father, I think, why I was so despondent.

DAVIS: Anaïs Nin, when she was here, talked a lot about the creative process in terms of neurosis, and the word *neurotic* was bandied about a lot. Do you think your anguish or your fears are realistic fears, or would you describe yourself as a neurotic?

DIDION: Well, at one point I would have described myself as a neurotic. I used to think of myself as a neurotic when I was in college. I think that was during a period when everybody was thinking of themselves as neurotic. I don't know now. I don't really think now in terms of neurosis. I think in terms of only extreme psychosis or normal—I mean, or you're getting along all right. Someone asked me last night why I had never gone into analysis because I was so shy, and I couldn't think what to say, and I said that, finally, I actually wouldn't want to go into analysis because if I found out too much about myself I might stop working, which is more important to me than being good at a dinner party.

DAVIS: Anaïs wrote, "I care very much about the human condition but I will not die from caring." Do you think ever, you're in danger, you feel like dying metaphorically from caring too much and being unable to continue therefore?

DIDION: No, not at this point, no.

DAVIS: Is it because you can put that caring into your work?

DIDION: Well, I think that everybody goes through a period of disgust—I don't mean disgust in terms of irritation but of kind of a moral disgust with everybody else's—with the way the world is and everything, and sometimes it seems pointless to write. But then you go through that to just working for yourself alone.

DAVIS: But there are times, for instance in the piece on Haight-Ashbury, when you're feeling that everything is falling apart and that the center cannot hold. It's so intense that one wonders how on earth you could feel as intensely as that and still stay together, and still stay functioning.

DIDION: Well, that's the trick. I mean, that's the way it's done. I mean, that was a period when I did feel that there was maybe not much point in writing, but just my sheer interest in the techniques of writing kept me going, and also I needed money.

DAVIS: The Linda Kasabian book is not coming out.

DIDION: No.

DAVIS: What are you going to do next?

DIDION: Well, I'm starting another novel. And I'm starting a nonfiction book. I don't know which—I'll do one for a while and then pick up the other.

DAVIS: Joan, thank you very much.

A VISIT WITH JOAN DIDION

INTERVIEW BY SARA DAVIDSON
THE NEW YORK TIMES BOOK REVIEW
APRIL 3, 1977

Her office is a chamber in which to dream waking dreams. It is a small, Spartan room where the curtains are always drawn. There are props and cue cards. While she worked on *A Book of Common Prayer*, a map of Central America hung on the wall. Set out on a table were postcards from Colombia, a newspaper photo of a janitor mopping up blood in a Caribbean hotel, books on tropical foliage and tropical medicine and a Viasa Airlines schedule with "Maracaibo-Paris" circled in blue. "Maracaibo-Paris—I thought those were probably the perimeters of the book," Joan Didion said.

I have been making the drive for six years and it never seems shorter: forty miles up the Pacific Coast Highway to Trancas, where Joan lives with her husband, John Gregory Dunne, and their daughter Quintana. Once past Malibu the landscape changes. Wild mustard and cactus grow on the hills, and the oceanfront is no longer a protected bay. It is a seacoast.

Joan enjoys "forms," and an evening in her home has a curve as carefully plotted as the narrative of one of her books. Orchids are placed about the room. Drinks are served by the fire. Joan wears a long dress, white thong sandals and a flower in her hair. Her sandals slapping on the tile, she walks to the kitchen where she completes preparations for dinner, consulting a menu written on a white pad:

Artichokes vinaigrette
Roast Loin of Pork w/ Orange Sauce
Corn Soufflé
Crème Caramel

On the Saturday in February when I drove out to
Trancas to conduct an interview with Joan, it was with
some apprehension. She is not what one would call a vir-
tuoso conversationalist. We taped four hours, of which she
said later, "two hours were pauses." As I set up the machine,
John Dunne wandered into the living room wearing a blue
bathrobe. "I got the Saturday jits," he said. "I got anxiety
crawling over me."

He asked Joan, "Do you have any Coke? Then I'll disappear, so I don't answer all your questions for you."

She brought him a Coca-Cola.

When John returned to his study, we settled on the
couch. Joan was wearing a light blue sweatshirt and faded
straight-leg jeans. Her reddish-blond hair was parted in the
center. She smoked Pall Malls, or twisted a blue rubber band
around her fingers, and at times her sentences trailed into a
soft, rapid laughter.

JOAN DIDION: How are we going to go about this, in terms of
talking naturally?

SARA DAVIDSON: There are a lot of things I know that I'm
going to ask anyway.

DIDION: So we'll do it like a regular interview.

DAVIDSON: Yes, I even have a list of questions. I figured that was the only way, otherwise . . .

DIDION: [*laughing*] . . . otherwise we'd end up cooking.

DAVIDSON: Could you talk about the origins of *A Book of Common Prayer*?

DIDION: In the spring of 1973, John and I went to Cartagena, Colombia, and the entire trip was like a hallucination, partly because I had a fever. It seemed to me extraordinary that North America had gone one way and South America had gone another and I couldn't understand why. I kept reading that they had more resources than we had, they had more of everything and yet they had gone another way.

DAVIDSON: How would you define the other way?

DIDION: Obviously they're not industrialized, that's one way. Also, in North America, social tensions that arise tend to be undercut and co-opted quite soon, but in Latin America there does not seem to be any political machinery for delaying the revolution. Everything is thrown into bold relief. There is a collapsing of time. Everything is both older than you could ever know, and it started this morning.

DAVIDSON: Did you read García Márquez's *One Hundred Years of Solitude*?

DIDION: Yes, it's so wonderful. I was overcome by the book when I read it, but when I went down there, I realized the book was far more social realism than it was fantasy. The element which had seemed to me fantastic was quite reportorial.

DAVIDSON: Did you have a technical intention for this book?

DIDION: Yes, I wrote it down on the map of Central America. "Surface like rainbow slick, shifting, fall, thrown away, iridescent." I wanted to do a deceptive surface that appeared to be one thing and turned color as you looked through it.

DAVIDSON: What about the repetitions of phrases?

DIDION: It seemed constantly necessary to remind the reader to make certain connections. Technically it's almost a chant. You could read it as an attempt to cast a spell, or come to terms with certain contemporary demons. I can't think what those demons are at the moment but there's a range: flash politics, sexual adventurism.

DAVIDSON: What has been your experience with politics?

DIDION: I never had faith that the answers to human problems lay in anything that could be called political. I thought the answers, if there were answers, lay someplace in man's soul. I have had an aversion to social action because it usually meant social regulation. It meant interference, rules, doing what other people wanted me to do. The ethic I was raised in was specifically a western frontier ethic. That means being left alone and leaving others alone. It is regarded by members of my family as the highest form of human endeavor.

DAVIDSON: Do you vote?

DIDION: Once in a while. I'm hardly ever conscious of issues. I mean they seem to me like ripples on an ocean. In the life of the body politic, the actual movement is going on underneath and I am interested in what's going on underneath. What *Life* magazine used to call "the quality of life in our time" is determined not by who is in the White House but by economic forces. The politics I personally want are anarchic. Throw out the laws. Tear it down. Start all over. That is very romantic because it presumes that left to their own devices, people would do good things for one another. I doubt that that's true. But I would like to believe it.

DAVIDSON: Do you feel identified with Charlotte and Grace in this book?

DIDION: I think you identify with all your characters. They become your family, closer to you than anybody you know. They kind of move into the house and take over the furniture. It's one of the difficult things about writing a book and leading a normal, social, domestic life.

DAVIDSON: What is the effect of seeing people and getting stimulation?

DIDION: It's quite destructive. Either you sit there and just close off, or if you do become engaged in what is going on with other people, then you have lost the thread. You've turned off the computer, and it is not for that period of time making the connections it ought to be making. I really started thinking of my mind mechanically. I almost heard a steady humming if it was working all right, but if it stopped for a couple of days then it would take a while to get it back.

DAVIDSON: In "Why I Write" [a lecture delivered at the University of California at Berkeley], there's a confidence expressed about the process of writing that I know you don't always feel.

DIDION: I didn't express confidence so much as blind faith that if you go in and work every day, it will get better. Three days will go by and you will be in that office and you will think every day is terrible. But on the fourth day, if you do go in, if you don't go into town or out in the garden, something usually will break through.

DAVIDSON: How do you feel when you wake up?

DIDION: Oh, I don't want to go in there at all. It's low dread, every morning. That dread goes away after you've been in there an hour. I keep saying "in there" as if it's some kind of chamber, a different atmosphere. It is in a way. There's almost a psychic wall. The air changes, I mean you don't want to go through that door. But once you're in there, you're there and it's hard to go out.

DAVIDSON: I'd always assumed that after you'd been writing for a number of years, that fear would disappear.

DIDION: No, it doesn't. It's a fear you're not going to get it right. You're going to ruin it. You're going to fail. The touchy part on a book—when there's not the dread in the morning, when there's the dread all day long—is before it takes. Once it takes, there's just the morning dread and the occasional three days of terrible stuff; but before it takes, there's nothing to guarantee that it's going to take. There's a point in a novel where it shifts gears or the narrative won't carry. That point has to come before a third of the way through. It goes into overdrive. There are some novels you pick up and start reading and they're wonderful. Maybe you have to go to lunch or something and you get to page seventy and never pick them up again. You're not moved to keep turning pages. That's the narrative curve you've got to allow, around page seventy or eighty, to give it enough thrust to send it out. Imagine a rocket taking off. There's a point at which it drops its glitter or glamour and starts floating free.

DAVIDSON: How do you feel about a book while you're writing it?

DIDION: I try to hold my opinion in suspension. I hate the book when I'm working on it. But if I gave way to that thought, I would never finish the book, and then I would feel depressed and useless and have nothing to do all day.

DAVIDSON: Have you ever not finished a book?

DIDION: I've put things aside at forty pages.

DAVIDSON: Did you get depressed?

DIDION: Yes. There's a certain euphoric mania at first, when you think you've made the right decision and are really taking charge, but it sort of lies there as something you haven't finished. And you always wonder if maybe you had pushed a little harder, it might have broken through. I mean it's a failure. So, starting anything, there's a great chance for psychic loss.

DAVIDSON: How did you feel after finishing *A Book of Common Prayer*?

DIDION: I was tired, so tired. I didn't want to read it. I haven't read it. I like it, though, in an abstract way. It's like a dream again.

DAVIDSON: I take it success and failure are important issues for you?

DIDION: Yes. I suppose they are. I don't want to do anything that I don't do well. I don't want to ski. [*laughs*]

DAVIDSON: What about tennis?

DIDION: I do play tennis, not well, but I've moved into

thinking of it as a way of getting color on my face and mild exercise, not as playing tennis. I haven't learned to serve yet. Every once in a while my teacher brings it up, but it takes too much coordination. He brought it up again last week and I was on the verge of tears. I was furious, because I was really hitting the ball across the net pretty well.

DAVIDSON: Could you talk about your writing method?

DIDION: When I started this book, I wrote the first paragraph and continued for about three pages. Then I got scared and started skipping around and writing odd things.

DAVIDSON: What did you get scared of?

DIDION: Scared I couldn't sustain it. So I started writing odd bits here and there, and then I stopped being scared, when I had a pile of little things that appeared to be in the same tone as the beginning of the book. I just went back and started writing straight through until about page forty. By then the book was taking a slightly different direction. It was clear there was a narrator, for example. I had not intended there to be a narrator. I was going to be the female author's voice. I the author was going to tell you the reader the story. But the "I" became so strong that it became a character, so I went back and rewrote those forty pages with that narrator. As the story developed, things kept changing, and you can push ahead for a little while knowing that those things are wrong back there but you can't push too far or you lose precision. It doesn't matter to you as much, if you know it's wrong back there, so I started over again. I started over about twelve times. I wanted to start over when I went to Sacramento to finish it, but I didn't have time.

DAVIDSON: You always go to Sacramento to finish your books. Is that a ritual?

DIDION: It's very easy for me to work there. My concentration can be total because nobody calls me. I'm not required to lead a real life. I'm like a child, in my parents' house.

DAVIDSON: Do you have a room there?

DIDION: Yes. It's sort of a carnation pink, and the vines and trees have grown up over the windows. It's exactly like a cave. It's a very safe place. It's a good room to work in; it's a finishing room. I once tried to work in John's office here and I was beside myself. There were too many books. I mean there was this weight of other people's opinions around me. I worked in the Faculty Club in Berkeley for a month, and it was very hard to work there because I didn't have the map of Central America. Not that Boca Grande is on the map, but the map took on a real life in my mind. I mean that very narrow isthmus. One of the things that worried me about this book was that there were several kinds of weather. It took place in San Francisco, the American South and Central America. This sounds silly, but I was afraid that the narrative wouldn't carry if the weather changed. You wouldn't walk away from the book remembering one thing. The thing I wanted you to walk away remembering was the Central American weather. So all the things I had around my office had to do with Central America.

DAVIDSON: Where did you get the title?

DIDION: It just seemed right. *A Book of Common Prayer* was very important to this book. Why, I had no idea. At one point, my editor, Henry Robbins, asked what the title meant. I made up some specious thing and told him. I don't remember what I told him, something to the effect that the whole thing was a prayer. You could say that this was Grace's prayer for Charlotte's soul. If you have a narrator, which suddenly I was stuck with, the narrator can't just be telling you a story, something that happened, to entertain you. The narrator has got to be telling you the story for a reason. I think the title probably helped me with that.

DAVIDSON: Are you as skeptical about religion as you are about politics?

DIDION: I am quite religious in a certain way. I was brought up Episcopalian, and I stopped going to church because I hated the stories. You know the story about the prodigal son? I have never understood that story. I have never understood why the prodigal son should be treated any better than the other son. I have missed the point of a lot of parables. I have much too literal and practical a mind, they just don't appeal to me, they irritate me. But I like the words of the Episcopal service, and I say them over and over in my mind. There's one particular phrase which is part of every service: "As it was in the beginning, is now, and ever shall be, world without end. Amen." It's a very comforting phrase to a child. And to an adult. I have a very rigid sense of right and wrong. What I mean is, I use the words all the time. Even the smallest things. A table can be right or wrong

DAVIDSON: What about behavior?

DIDION: Behavior is right or wrong. I was once having dinner with a psychiatrist who told me that I had monocular vision, and there was no need for everything to be right or wrong. Well, that way lies madness. In order to maintain a semblance of purposeful behavior on this earth, you have to believe that things are right or wrong.

DAVIDSON: What authors have influenced you?

DIDION: As far as influence on a style goes, I don't think you're influenced by anybody you read after age twenty. That all happens before you start working yourself. You would never know it from reading me, but I was very influenced by Hemingway when I was thirteen, fourteen, fifteen. I learned a lot about how sentences worked. How a short sentence worked in a paragraph, how a long sentence worked. Where the commas worked. How every word had to matter. It made me excited about words. Conrad, for the same reasons. The sentences sounded wonderful. I remember being so excited once, when I discovered that the key lines in *Heart* *of Darkness* were in parentheses. James, whom I didn't read until I was in college, was important to me in trying to come to terms with the impossibility of getting it right. James's sentences, with all those clauses, had to do with keeping the options open, letting the sentence cover as much as it could. That impressed me a great deal.

DAVIDSON: What determines what you read now?

DIDION: When I'm working I don't read much at all. If it's a good book it will depress me because mine isn't as good. If it's a bad book it will depress me because mine's just as bad. I don't want anybody else's speech rhythms in my dream. I never read *Ragtime* [by E. L. Doctorow]. I opened the first page and saw it had a very strong rhythm, so I just put it away like a snake.

DAVIDSON: There's a certain aesthetic to the way you live. You once talked about using good silver every day.

DIDION: Well, every day is all there is.

DAVIDSON: Do you admire elegance?

DIDION: Yes, because it makes you feel better. It's a form. I'm very attached to certain forms, little compulsive rituals. I like to cook; I like to sew. They're peaceful things, and they're an expression of caring.

DAVIDSON: Could you talk about what you refer to as your shyness?

DIDION: I'm not particularly sociable. I like a lot of people, and I'm glad to see them, but I don't give the impression of being there. Part of it is that I'm terribly inarticulate. A sentence doesn't occur to me as a whole thing unless I'm working.

DAVIDSON: Isn't it a surprise to people who read you and expect the same fluency in your conversation?

DIDION: I don't know what they expect but they certainly don't get it. [*laughs*] I don't know why, and I don't know what I can do about it, and it is easier for me to just write it off and try to do better at what I do well.

DAVIDSON: I once asked if you liked living in Trancas and you said you found it a hostile environment.

DIDION: The only really benign climate I've ever been in is Hawaii. All other climates strike me as hostile.

DAVIDSON: What makes Hawaii benign and Cartagena, Colombia, not?

DIDION: In the Caribbean, there is rot, real rot. Hawaii is a tropic without rot.

DAVIDSON: Are you sure?

DIDION: Well, there's mildew. The place just strikes me as benign. It is sweet, it smells pink to me, it smells like flowers.

It is a pink environment and it makes me feel good. This is an arid environment. This is a desert. There's cactus growing across the highway. If the cactus started on that slope going down to the ocean—I think about it all the time, about the cactus coming across the Pacific Coast Highway and starting on that slope. I don't like the desert. I don't like dryness. I like everything to be wet.

DAVIDSON: What was your fantasy, then, about owning land in Nevada?

DIDION: It was the last place where you could have enough land so that as far as you could see, you owned it. It was relatively cheap. Land in southern Nevada was selling as recently as five years ago for three dollars an acre, in nine-hundred-thousand-acre pieces. Obviously you couldn't grow anything on it, you couldn't graze on it, but as far as you could see, it was yours. Nobody else could come on it.

DAVIDSON: What would you do on it?

DIDION: Just look out. [*laughs*]

DAVIDSON: Is it important for you to live near the ocean?

DIDION: I don't think so. I like the horizon out there. I like the flatness, which is the same flatness you get if you're looking out on nine hundred thousand acres in southern Nevada. There's a straight line across there and it's easy to keep your bearings. But I hardly ever go down to the beach.

DAVIDSON: Why?

DIDION: Well, usually I'm working.

DAVIDSON: Is John your editor?

DIDION: Yes, we edit each other. A lot of people wonder how we can edit each other and live together, but it works out very well. We trust each other. Sometimes we don't agree. Obviously you never want to agree when somebody tells you something doesn't work. I don't mean that kind of not agreeing. That's just when you're tired and it's midnight. I mean, sometimes, even on reflection, we don't agree, and there is a tacit understanding that neither of us will push too far. Each of us is aware that it would be easy to impose our sensibility, particularly our own style, on each other. And so there is a tacit agreement not to push beyond saying, "It doesn't work. This is how to fix it." If there is still a substantive disagreement it's never mentioned again.

DAVIDSON: Are you more interested in writing fiction these days than nonfiction?

DIDION: I'm trying to do a nonfiction book now. I have always sort of wanted to write a book about California water. I'm interested in water—the pipes that water goes through, the mechanics of getting the water from place to place. I could look at a flume all day. I love dams, the way they are almost makes me weak, it's so beautiful.

There's a thing they do on the water project that I would

like so much to see, that I've never had any reason to set up an appointment to go and see. Farmers, say, in the Imperial Valley, order their water ahead. You have to put in your order the week or the night before, and then there's a ditch rider who goes down the ditch and opens the valves to each ranch, and lets a certain amount of water go through. Technically that interests me. I don't know what I could do with it. Maybe I would like to be the person who opens the valves and lets the water through. Because it interests me and all I know how to do is write, I have thought about writing a book about California water, but I have mentioned it to a few people in New York and they have not been terribly interested.

DAVIDSON: You could have chosen to live anywhere. New York, the South. Did you pick Los Angeles because you think it's interesting?

DIDION: I love it here. It has a kind of energy I like and a kind of inertia I like. It's a very good place to work. The weather's all right, and the place is neutral, it has for me no social overtones whatsoever.

DAVIDSON: Do you like to drive?

DIDION: No, I can't stand it. I hardly ever drive. People are always calling me up for a quote on the freeways. I could probably number on both hands the times I've driven freeways. I can only enter a freeway if it's at the beginning. I can't enter it at a normal entrance or I freeze, like a child at the top of a slide. Freeways are so tricky for me that I am obsessed by them.

When I've driven one, I think I've really flown the Atlantic, gone to the moon, and I replay it in my mind: exactly what lane I was in and where the crossover was. The two pages about the freeway in *Play It as It Lays* came out of that obsession.

DAVIDSON: Are you intrigued by the movie community?

DIDION: It interests me as an industry; you can watch it working. I like following the moves of the particular game. I like movie people. If I lived in Detroit, I would want to see automotive people. I would want to know what the moves were.

DAVIDSON: Why do you write for movies?

DIDION: One reason, obviously, is for the money. It's specious to say you could make the same amount of money writing a book. You can't write a book every year, but you have to keep on living every year. A lot of writers support themselves by teaching and lecturing. I don't like to do that. It uses up far more energy.

DAVIDSON: What about the frustrations—deals falling through?

DIDION: If your whole conception of yourself depended on whether or not you got a movie going, you might as well go up to San Francisco and get sad and jump. But ours doesn't. Our real life is someplace else. It's sort of a game. Also, it's very gratifying; it's fun, at least a first draft is fun. It's not like writing, it's like doing something else.

DAVIDSON: Do you think it's proper or feasible to write about sex in an explicit way?

DIDION: I don't think anything is improper in fiction, that there's any area that can't be dealt with. I don't in point of fact know very many people who deal with sex well. The only person who deals with sex in an explicit way whom I can read without being made profoundly uncomfortable is Norman Mailer. I know that's not an opinion shared by many. Mailer deals with sex in a very clean, direct way. There's no sentimentality around it. He takes it seriously. I tend to deal with sex obliquely. There is a lot of sexual content in *Common Prayer*, there was quite a lot in *Play It as It Lays* too, but it was underneath. I'm just more comfortable dealing with it as an undertone.

DAVIDSON: Some people complain that your female characters are passive drifters who lead purposeless lives. Do you see Charlotte Douglas that way?

DIDION: No, I don't see that about any women I've written about. I think there is a confusion between passive and successful. Passive simply mean passive, and active means active. Active doesn't necessarily imply success. Charlotte is very much in control there in Boca Grande when everyone else is running out. She knows just what she's doing.

DAVIDSON: She doesn't seem to have a center, something in herself for which she's living.

DIDION: Obviously the book finds her at a crisis. I don't know too many people who have what you could call clearly functioning centers.

DAVIDSON: You have your work, that sustains you no matter what. And devotion to your family.

DIDION: They could all fall apart tomorrow. This is not a problem peculiar to women, it is a problem for all of us to find something at the center. Charlotte finds her center in Boca Grande. She finds her life by leaving it. I think most of us build elaborate structures to fend off spending much time in our own center.

DAVIDSON: Do you think of yourself as sad or depressed?

DIDION: No, I think of myself as really happy. Cheerful. I'm always amazed at what simple things can make me happy. I'm really happy every night when I walk past the windows and the evening star comes out. A star of course is not a simple thing, but it makes me happy. I look at it for a long time. I'm always happy, really.

DAVIDSON: How do you feel about getting older?

DIDION: I'm a very slow writer and I could count, if I wanted to—which I don't—the number of books I will have time to write. I work more. I work harder. There is a sense of urgency now.

JOAN DIDION IMMERSES HERSELF INTO THE MAELSTROM

INTERVIEW BY MARTIN TORGOFF
INTERVIEW
JUNE 1, 1983

In June of 1982, Joan Didion travelled to El Salvador with her husband, John Gregory Dunne, to report on the country for *The New York Review of Books*. The results of that trip appeared as three articles, and were published in book form last month by Simon and Schuster. To readers familiar with the work of this highly acclaimed essayist, critic, reporter, novelist, and scenarist, the trip made a great deal of sense; the region had obviously been on her mind for some time. *A Book of Common Prayer*, her novel published in 1978, prophetically depicted the downfall of a Somoza-like regime in the imaginary Central American nation of Boca Grande, which bore a startling resemblance to Nicaragua. Moreover, it seemed reasonable to assume that if any writer could get a handle on El Salvador—caught, as it is, in the throes of a savage civil war, as the newly unleashed anti-Sandinist insurgency in Nicaragua causes tensions in the region to mount, at a time when the political atmosphere of the United States is charged by issues of human rights violations by the Salvadoran Right and the question of increased U.S. military aid—it would be Joan Didion.

After reading the book, one thing became searingly clear: What has always informed Didion's nonfiction in the past and distinguished *Slouching Towards Bethlehem* and *The White Album* as classics—a sensitivity that is viscerally sensitive, vulnerable yet always tough-minded, an unerringly keen eye for detail and irony, and a prose style of singular brilliance—only makes *Salvador* that much more devastating. Perhaps the most telling phrases she uses in the book to describe her impressions are those like "a prolonged amnesiac fugue" and "a true noche obscura"—in other words, there is no "handle" in El Salvador; there is mainly the ambition for power—("Don't say this, but, there are no issues here," she is told by a high placed Salvadoran. "There are only ambitions.")—obfuscated by the rhetoric of "*el problema*," "*la situacion*," "*la verdad*," "*la solucion*." Mostly there is "the exact mechanism of terror" she comes to understand so well; there are El Playon and Puerta del Diablo, where the mutilated bodies of the "*desaparecidos*" are dumped by the death squads, and the kind of "practical information" she imparts at the outset of the book:

> In El Salvador, one learns that the vultures go first for the soft tissue, for the eyes, the exposed genitalia, the open mouth. One learns that an open mouth can be used to make a specific point, can be stuffed with something emblematic; stuffed, say, with a penis, or, if the point has to do with land title, stuffed with some of the dirt in question.

"Terror is the given of the place," she tells us, terror and death are the true tangibles in El Salvador—the rest is rhetoric, illusion. Seated across from her in a suite at The Carlyle, what comes immediately to mind upon meeting her is how physically ill-suited she seems, at first glance, to encounter such dark forces. For Joan Didion is not simply diminutive but somehow, despite her strong-looking hands and her intense, steady blue eyes, profoundly fragile—a pale, thin, gentle wisp of a woman, with chestnut hair and a soft western twang. She could seemingly be blown clear across the room by a strong breeze . . . the fact that she has chosen to immerse herself into the maelstrom of El Salvador only makes her accomplishment all the more remarkable and compelling.

MARTIN TORGOFF: Why did you write the kind of book you did? You obviously decided to concentrate on reporting about the "texture" of life in El Salvador, what it's like to live in that environment; but at the same time, you seem to have eschewed what people in the State Department might call "the big picture," i.e. the Russians, the Cubans, the Nicaraguans, the question of geopolitics.

JOAN DIDION: Every once in a while, it filters into the writing, but no, I didn't want to concentrate on that. I was aware of what I was doing: I didn't think that "the big picture" was necessary because I don't think we understand what it is. And so many people have been telling us what "the big picture" is all too often; I wasn't agreeing with what they were portraying, I wanted my impressions of things to speak for themselves.

TORGOFF: When you were down there, did you find your movement restricted by the situation?

DIDION: No, not really; we could go anywhere. There were always roadblocks, and if you didn't have the right papers, things could have always ended badly. We were very careful to carry our papers from the Ministry of Defense identifying us as members of the press. There were days when we'd have to stop because the rebels would periodically burn cars and trucks on the roads.

TORGOFF: Was it just you and your husband traveling? Did you have a guide?

DIDION: We didn't have a guide; we just rented a car and went out. Sometimes we went out with other reporters. We tried to get around as best as we could.

TORGOFF: You use the word "disappeared" in the book, describing its usage down there: someone is "disappeared" when they are abducted and most of those "disappeared" are tortured, killed and mutilated. Didn't it seem plausible that it could have happened to both of you?

DIDION: We thought it wasn't going to happen because someone always knew where we were when we were going out . . . But, in hindsight, I realize that it doesn't really make much difference if someone knows where you are, does it? When you're actually there, you try to be very careful but it doesn't pay to think about it too much; you're there to do a job and you can't let the fear stop you from making your rounds. But, you're always aware of it. I remember the first night we were there, we were with a bunch of reporters and the first thing I noticed was that everyone sits facing the door.

TORGOFF: You saw a lot of grisly things down there—the

body pits, the morgue. We can read about these things in the paper, perhaps even see it on television, but the reality still seems remote. Does having seen those things alter your perceptions of things?

DIDION: Yes, when we first came back last summer from El Salvador, I remember landing in New York; I found it astonishing, outside the terminal these two cabdrivers were having an argument, a fight . . . they were shouting at each other, nothing more. But after El Salvador, I was so shocked that I wanted to run and hide, just because that for this very short period of time—two weeks—I'd been in a situation where those sort of raised voices could have meant death. It was deeply shocking people, talk about the violence of New York. It's a luxury here.

TORGOFF: You evoke the element of incomprehension in the book—you use the word "untranslatable." Does that mean we, for instance, as Americans, with our values and perspectives cannot really perceive what's happening down there because it's not within our frame of reference?

DIDION: I don't think it's possible to get it unless you're there. For example, we keep waiting for the trial of the Guardsmen for the killing of four American nuns. What I'm really saying is that it's as inconceivable for the Guardsmen to be brought to justice down there, as it seems inconceivable up here for them not to be. Things are really bad down there and the minute somebody tries to tell you about them, they put it into a rational framework. When I say that they rationalize,

I mean that just the act of telling it makes it seem more rational. There's no way to actually tell it. When, for example, something happens down there, a lot of it turns up in the embassy reporting; it looks more rational in a cable to the State Department than it actually is. And then when a State Department spokesman translates it, he rationalizes it one step further. And by the time it reaches us here, it's entirely transformed; it seems rational when it's not.

TORGOFF: I wonder how that applies to our opinions, whether you're a liberal Democrat or a conservative Republican. If the reality is divorced from our experience as a people, is it reasonable to expect to be able to impose any of our institutions or ideals on the situation? What I'm getting at is this: If the situation is inherently "untranslatable" then how can we possibly know what to do?

DIDION: I don't think we can with any certainty now. It's unrealistic to expect to export our values, our political abstracts. The abstracts that we live by don't even apply. We're seriously deluding ourselves by our present course. It has no possibility for a good outcome; it's against our interests. We're defeating our best interests there.

TORGOFF: What are our own best interests there, as you perceive them?

DIDION: Our best long-term interests are to have friends in our own hemisphere, to have the respect and support of other countries. What we seem to be doing is driving them away, one by one, isolating ourselves. We, in effect, are making ourselves a Fortress America—it's not the Soviets doing it—it's us. If you assume that the Soviet Union wants us isolated in our own hemisphere, wants us in effect to become a lone fortress, we are helping them in every possible way. That's what I mean by self-defeating.

TORGOFF: Is what's happening in El Salvador primarily a class conflict between the haves and the have-nots?

DIDION: I see it more as a conflict within a class. Some people see it as a popular revolution—it has elements of that, but I don't think it was, originally. There's a conflict among people who are already entitled—the haves: the traditional oligarchy and the subclass of professionals, army officers, and the businessmen, who aren't necessarily owners of vast wealth or property.

TORGOFF: In other words, there's a conflict within the elite of the society, between those who are trying to call the shots?

DIDION: Trying to call the shots . . . and one of their points of conflict is how to deal with those at the bottom. I can't get much more specific than that; I don't go into it in the book—somebody should go into it, however. It's a conflict between those who have power and those who want it, or have less power, or are temporarily out of power. That's what began the revolution in Nicaragua: there were people who were powerful families, but who weren't the Somozas . . . It became a popular revolution later.

TORGOFF: Why do you think that the guerillas, being out-numbered and outgunned, do so well against the army in El Salvador?

DIDION: Militarily? Well, I'm no expert, but the United States seems to find a great deal to be desired in the morale and tactics of the Salvadoran army. They keep sending these three battalions hurtling across the country like ping-pong balls; the guerillas just fade back into the hills and disappear. And then these three battalions just rush off someplace else and the guerillas come back out.

TORGOFF: Isn't it true that the average Salvadoran soldier, the grunt who has to go slogging off into the bush, is from the same class as the guerillas?

DIDION: Yes, they have no interest in the war; they couldn't possibly. It's chance: if you're of the right age and you're picked up in an army sweep, you're in the army; if they miss you and the guerillas come to your town, then you can just as easily be a guerilla. There have been documented instances of army officers selling weapons and supplies to the guerillas—it's very murky. But there certainly isn't high morale in the Salvadoran army.

TORGOFF: One hears a good deal about the terror tactics of the government security forces, of course. Are the guerillas guilty of the same terror? For instance, in Vietnam, the Vietcong were known to enter a village, round up the boys and tell them that if they didn't join up they'd blow their fathers' brains out . . .

DIDION: Certainly, the guerillas do a lot of terrorism—I don't know if they do that, however—I really don't know. A lot of people have reported about their public relations, however, which appears to be quite effective—taking the people they capture and feeding them well, turning them loose. It's very demoralizing to the army.

TORGOFF: If the government of El Salvador gets the military aid it wants, what do you see happening?

DIDION: Business as usual. It would be like supporting a bankrupt business buying little amounts of time so that nobody has to become the weapon who "lost" El Salvador.

TORGOFF: Now look at the reverse angle: If we cut off aid, will the guerillas "shoot their way into power," to put it in the words of Secretary of State Shultz?

DIDION: It's really hard to say . . . I presume what would happen would be that the Right would have to revert to shooting everybody in the country and trying to solve the problem that way . . . What would happen if we cut off aid? Maybe some of the money that left El Salvador in 1979, when the rich families left for Miami, might come back. Some $2 billion was taken out of the country that year.

TORGOFF: So if we stopped the aid, we would become powerless, in effect, to influence the course of events there?

DIDION: But we're giving the money and we're powerless to influence the course of events now. I think we should encourage a negotiated solution, negotiated regionally with countries like Mexico and Venezuela participating, rather than seeking an armed solution.

TORGOFF: If there are serious negotiations of elections in which the Left agrees to participate, do you think that the people in power in El Salvador would ever actually share it with the Left? Or, for that matter, would they share it with the center—if there is a center?

DIDION: I don't think they would ever share it with the Left; they haven't even been willing to share it with the center. They've been systematically killing off the Christian Democrats . . . the Right hasn't been willing to share power with anybody in El Salvador. Period.

TORGOFF: As far as other nonfiction you've done over the years, was this a particularly difficult book to write?

DIDION: No, it was easier. Basically, I started out to write an article, or a series of articles, and it kept getting longer. It was easier to write than all of the things I've written because I was very clear about what I saw, what I thought. I just set out to put it down without any embellishments or tricks.

TORGOFF: More and more novelists seem to be seizing on Central American settings for their own purposes. I'm thinking of your novel, *A Book of Common Prayer*, Robert Stone's

A Flag for Sunrise, and Paul Theroux's *The Mosquito Coast.* What is there about the place that attracts the imagination of the American novelist?

DIDION: It's an interesting question. It reminds me of that woman last night. [On the previous night, Didion gave a talk on El Salvador at the Overseas Press Club in New York.] There was an Italian journalist who'd been to El Salvador who raised a point about American reporters there. She used the phrase "moral ambiguity" and said that the American reporters seemed to be getting something "out of it." What she was sort of getting at, I think, was that Americans have a very peculiar relationship to Central America. We have a history in Central America—it hasn't really been a history we should be applauded for. It's been a rather mysterious chapter for us. It's been kind of a frontier for us; a lot of Americans have gone down there, for many different reasons. It makes me think of this classic first line in a bad novel: "I came up from Central America traveling fast . . ."

TORGOFF: When you get right down to it, would you say that they just don't like the gringos down there?

DIDION: That's exactly right: The Right in El Salvador doesn't like us at all. They don't want any strings attached to our money; they resent us trying to tell them what to do. I don't know how the Left feels about us. Should the Left prevail, however, we're more or less guaranteeing, by our support of the Right, a government hostile to us, which is, of course, what happened in Nicaragua.

TORGOFF: So it's a no-win situation: We're damned if we do, and damned if we don't?

DIDION: That's right.

TORGOFF: I want to read you the first sentence of a review of *Salvador* in the *Daily News*. I thought you might find it amusing, knowing your reputation for being, shall we say, saturnine. It's by a fellow named David Hinckley—no relation, I presume to the presidential assailant: "Joan Didion is a writer who would find something melancholy in the Resurrection . . ."

DIDION: [*laughs*] Oh, no! Well, I'm so tired of that stuff—I'm really tired of this angst business. It seems to me I'm as lively and cheerful as the next person. I laugh, I smile . . . but I write down what I see. There have been reviews of *Salvador* that have said I found it so depressing because I find everything so depressing. I would like to know how they would find it? After all, what do they think is down there?

THE SALON
INTERVIEW

INTERVIEW BY DAVE EGGERS
SALON
OCTOBER 28, 1996

Joan Didion's new novel, *The Last Thing He Wanted*, is her first in twelve years. Set in 1984, it centers on Elena McMahon, an American journalist who gets tangled up in the covert sales of American arms in Central America. It is sparely written and tightly plotted and fiercely intelligent—all the sorts of things we've come to expect from Didion.

Some things that you probably know but if not will be helpful in enjoying this interview:

- Didion is married to John Gregory Dunne, and has been for a long time. When she says "we," he makes "we."
- Though she no longer writes the sort of personal-social essays that made up books like *The White Album* and *Slouching Towards Bethlehem*, she still contributes journalism and critical essays to magazines like *The New Yorker* and *The New York Review of Books*.
- In person she is very small. She is also graceful, personable, warm and funny.

DAVE EGGERS: With *The Last Thing He Wanted*, I read that you weren't sure how it was going to turn out until you were finished with it.

JOAN DIDION: No, no I wasn't. I wanted to do a very, very tight plot, just a single thread—you wouldn't even see the thread and then when you pulled it at the end everything would fall into place. That was the intention there. But you would go mad if you tried to plot that closely ahead of time. So essentially what you have to do, I found, is you have to make it up every day as you go along. And then you have to play the cards you already have on the table—you have to deal with what you've already said. Quite often, you've got yourself into things that seem to lead nowhere, but if you force yourself to deal with them, that was the discipline of it.

For example, one of the first things I had started with in this book was the idea of this woman walking off a campaign. Because I'd covered some campaigns in '88 and '92, I wanted to use some of that sense of a campaign. So then, I didn't know, then she would go to Miami to see her father. Then, I couldn't figure out where she'd been. Then I decided she ought to be from Los Angeles and had been married to someone in the oil business. That kind of gave me a fresh start. But then I was having to get her from Los Angeles to being a political reporter, right? It was a really hard thing to do. It was also a lot of fun.

EGGERS: There were certain chapters where it does sound like you're starting from scratch almost, when you start hearing about Elena's dreams, for example.

DIDION: Yeah, I mean, I was just sitting there wondering what I could do that day. Sometimes, also, you just feel it's right to step back from it a little bit. Otherwise it's going to get linear, "and then she said, and then she did . . ." It doesn't keep you awake to write it.

EGGERS: While your fiction seems to be getting increasingly lean, your essays seem to be moving in the opposite direction.

DIDION: They're getting denser and denser. There's a whole lot of stuff going on in a piece—you're trying to think it through. Generally, you think about a question or a situation in a more complex way than you would make a scene. Novels are almost like music or poetry—they just come to me in simple sentences, whereas I think my pieces get more and more complex ever since I've started using a computer.

EGGERS: What do you use?

DIDION: I use an IBM ThinkPad. I just use it like a typewriter, but when I started using it in 1987, I thought I won't be able to write anymore, so I thought I'd go back to the typewriter. But you couldn't go back to the typewriter after using the computer, so finally after about a month I got proficient enough that I could actually work on it without being distracted by it, and in fact then it started making me a whole lot more logical than I ever had been. Because the computer was so logical, it was always right, I was wrong . . . and the time saved.

Before I started working on a computer, writing a piece would be like making something up every day, taking the material and never quite knowing where you were going to go

next with the material. With a computer it was less like painting and more like sculpture, where you start with a block of
something and then start shaping it.

EGGERS: You feel like it's just there . . .

DIDION: It's just there, and sometimes you'll find yourself—
you get one paragraph partly right, and then you'll go back
and work on the other part. It's a different thing.

EGGERS: Your work feels like it was written by a slow writer.
I mean that in the best possible way.

DIDION: Over the course of several years I had false starts on
this novel several times. I couldn't get anywhere with it. Then
I had this block of time last fall from the end of August until
Christmas, so I just decided I would try to finish it in that
period. So I went back and I started, and I did finish it about
Christmastime, but that was about as fast as I could work.
And a lot of it turned out to already be done in note form to
hang together. So this was just running it through with the
thread.

EGGERS: There is a character in the book named Bob Weir.
Are you a Grateful Dead fan?

DIDION: [*laughs*] No, that is where that name comes from,
isn't it? I had totally forgotten that. No, I had no idea; I knew
there was something just right about that name.

EGGERS: Elena resembles, in certain ways, some of your other characters from some of your other novels, in that she finds herself in the middle of this huge life change, and it's seemingly irreversible, and yet she goes with it. What does that pattern mean to you?

DIDION: I don't know; it's nothing I want to examine too closely. Every time I do it, I think it's brand new. It comes to me in a flash! [*laughs*] It would certainly make things easier if I remembered, but it's—I guess all novels are dreams of what might happen or dreams of what you don't want to happen. When you're working on them, it's very much like a dream you're moving in. So, to some extent, obviously, the same characters are going to keep populating your dreams.

EGGERS: Have you ever done something like Elena does here—walked off a campaign, reinvented yourself?

DIDION: Not really, no. But you can see the possibility; it's something you might be afraid of happening. It's definitely something you don't want to happen. *I* don't want to happen. That's what I would take from it.

EGGERS: I read somewhere that you identified yourself as a libertarian.

DIDION: I was explaining to somebody what kind of Republican I had been. That was essentially why I had been feeling estranged from the Republican Party per se, because my whole point of view had been libertarian. I mean, I wouldn't call it totally "on the program" libertarian.

EGGERS: You don't vote the ticket?

DIDION: [*laughs*] No . . . I think the attraction was that it was totally free. It was totally based on individual rights, which, as a Westerner, I was responsive to. Then I started realizing there was a lot of ambiguity in the West's belief that it had a stronghold on rugged individualism, since basically it was created by the federal government. So I haven't come to any hard conclusion, here.

EGGERS: Are you watching the campaign? What do you think of Clinton?

DIDION: Well, he's the luckiest man alive, isn't he? He seems to be lucky, which I guess in a lot of cultures has been what people wanted. Luck had a kind of totemic power; that made you the leader.

EGGERS: I read your review of Bob Woodward's *The Choice*, in *The New York Review of Books*. It seemed that his lengthy descriptions of his reporterly methods got under your skin.

DIDION: Yes. There's a certain kind of reporting of a book that when you're casually reading through you think you've missed something, you're not informed here, you've totally missed the point, there must be something more to this than meets the eye. So then I started reading *The Choice* and I had been actually following the campaign in a way until then, so I did know something about it, and I thought, "What's going on here?" There's nothing here we don't know. And even then, I would sort of doze off every now and then and think, "I must be missing this—there must be more to this than I'm finding."

EGGERS: You and your husband wrote the screenplay for *Up Close and Personal.* How do you think it turned out?

DIDION: Well, it turned out—from the beginning, what it was supposed to be was a vehicle for two movie stars, and that's what it was.

EGGERS: You have no illusions, it seems, about the Hollywood game.

DIDION: Well, if you don't know how to play it you shouldn't be in it. It's always sort of amused me.

EGGERS: I just read an interview with Charles Schulz, the creator of *Peanuts.* He's a billionaire, of course, and he was asked what his idea of success was—if he considered himself "successful." He said something like, "Yes, because now I feel like I can go into any bookstore, and if I see a book I really like, I can buy it." I thought that was really beautiful. Do you consider yourself successful?

WRITING A STORY AFTER AN ENDING

INTERVIEW BY TERRY GROSS
FRESH AIR
OCTOBER 13, 2005

TERRY GROSS: "Life changes fast. Life changes in the instant. You sit down to dinner and life as you know it ends." Those are the first words of Joan Didion's new memoir, *The Year of Magical Thinking*. It's about the year following the death of her husband, the writer John Gregory Dunne. He died as they were sitting down to dinner on the night of December 30, 2003. It was a heart attack. He was seventy-one. Didion and Dunne had just come back from the hospital where their daughter was in a coma, suffering from pneumonia and septic shock. While Didion's memoir chronicles her grief for her husband, it also describes her daughter's medical progress and setbacks. By the close of her book, Didion thought her daughter was recovering, but just a few weeks ago in late August, she died from an abdominal infection. She was thirty-nine. Devastating is the way *New York Times* book critic Michiko Kakutani describes Didion's memoir.

Didion's best-known books include *Slouching Towards Bethlehem*, *Play It as It Lays*, and *A Book of Common Prayer*. Let's start with a reading from *The Year of Magical Thinking*. It begins as Didion and her husband were beginning dinner and what turned out to be his final moments.

JOAN DIDION: [*reading*] We sat down. My attention was on mixing the salad.

John was talking, then he wasn't.

At one point in the seconds or minute before he stopped talking he had asked me if I had used single-malt Scotch for his second drink. I had said no, I had used the same Scotch I had used for his first drink. 'Good,' he had said. 'I don't know why but I don't think you should mix them.' At another point in those seconds or that minute he had been talking about why World War One was the critical event from which the entire rest of the twentieth century flowed.

I have no idea which subject we were on, the Scotch or World War One, at the instant he stopped talking.

I only remember looking up. His left hand was raised and he was slumped motionless. At first I thought he was making a failed joke, an attempt to make the difficulty of the day seem manageable.

I remember saying *Don't do that.*

When he did not respond my first thought was that he had started to eat and choked. I remember trying to lift him far enough from the back of the chair to give him the Heimlich. I remember the sense of his weight as he fell forward, first against the table, then to the floor. In the kitchen by the phone I had taped a card with the New York–Presbyterian ambulance numbers. I had not taped the numbers by the phone because I anticipated a moment like this. I had taped the numbers by the phone in case someone in the building needed an ambulance.

Someone else.

I called one of the numbers. A dispatcher asked if he was breathing. I said *Just come.*

GROSS: That's Joan Didion reading from her new memoir, *The Year of Magical Thinking.*

Joan Didion, welcome to *Fresh Air.* And I just want to say at the top . . .

DIDION: Thank you.

GROSS: . . . I'm very sorry about the loss of your husband and your daughter. This is a really beautifully written book, and I loved reading it, but I also hated reading it, only in the sense that, you know, it makes me think not only of your losses; it makes me think of, you know, losses I may experience and losses—do you know what—it's . . .

DIDION: You know, I had the sense when I was writing it . . .

GROSS: Yeah.

DIDION: . . . that I wasn't writing it at all. It was like automatic writing. It's a very different kind of process. It was simply very—everything that I—was on my mind just came out and got on the page, and that was kind of my intention, to keep it kind of raw, because I thought that—it occurred to me, when I was doing a lot of reading about death and grief, that nobody told you the raw part. And every one of us is going to face it sooner or later.

GROSS: How do you think it affected your grieving, to be chronicling it as it happened?

DIDION: Well, it's the way I process everything, by writing it down. I don't actually process anything until I write it down, I mean, in terms of thinking, in terms of coming to terms with it. So it was kind of a necessary thing for me. I don't know that it would be for everybody. You have to actually probably be a writer to process that way.

GROSS: After you called, you know, 911, it took about five minutes for them to come. What did you . . .

DIDION: I didn't know—what did I do?

GROSS: Yeah. What'd you do in that five minutes?

DIDION: I kept trying to wake him up, and I kept trying to lift him. I kept trying to—I don't remember. I mean, I kept—I don't remember what I did. I didn't do anything. I mean, it was nothing—I remember calling downstairs and asking the doorman to come up, but actually the ambulance was there almost immediately.

GROSS: You had an autopsy done because you wanted to know, like, did he die, that moment he stopped talking, or . . .

DIDION: Yes, I wanted to know when he died, if I could have kept him alive.

GROSS: Were you feeling guilty that there was something you should have been able to do?

DIDION: I think everybody who has somebody die in their family feels guilty, because most of us think we should be omnipotent, that we should be able to control almost everything, you know. I mean, it's a delusion, but we do think that we should be able to keep those we love alive.

GROSS: Did the autopsy put your mind at ease on that count?

DIDION: It did. It was—the autopsy was surprising to me, because once I knew he'd had a heart attack, I assumed it was an arrhythmia of some kind, that he'd gone into ventricular fibrillation spontaneously or just because of an electrical malfunction. That wasn't the case. He died of coronary artery disease, which nobody—everybody had discounted, because he'd had it in 1987, had been treated for it. Everything looked fine. He would have annual tests, including an angiogram, and nothing ever showed. It was totally silent.

GROSS: Your book is called *The Year of Magical Thinking*, and you realized at some point that you had been engaging in magical thinking that had to do with this genuine thought that maybe he'd come back, so you shouldn't throw out his shoes in case he needs them when he comes back, and . . .

DIDION: Right. Maybe if I did the right things, he would come back. You know, it's a form—it's the way children think. A lot of people have told me, who have lost a husband or child, that they engaged in it, too.

GROSS: Is there a point where you realized you stopped?

DIDION: There was a point where I realized that I had been doing it, and yes, then I realized that, that gradually stopped. I don't think I'm doing it now.

GROSS: You talk about how you didn't want to give away his shoes, for example, because if he came back, he'd needed them.

DIDION: Right.

GROSS: Giving away clothes after someone dies is so hard. I mean, you have to decide with all their possessions: What are you going to keep? What are you going to give away to friends? What are you going to give to charity? What are you going to throw out? Was that a really horrible process?

DIDION: I haven't done it. I just left everything. After I discovered that I couldn't give away the shoes, I just closed that door. Now I haven't had to move or repaint the apartment or do anything that required me to do it. I think I presume that it would be somewhat less painful now than it was in the first few months, you know, when I initially tried it, because now I know he's dead in a way that I viscerally didn't know then.

But I would just as soon let that door stay closed for a while until I need to open it.

GROSS: If you're just joining us, my guest is Joan Didion, and she's written a memoir about the year after her husband's death. It's called *The Year of Magical Thinking*. And her husband was the writer John Gregory Dunne.

How much had you talked about death with your husband, and did you have those conversations about what to do if the other dies, and what you'd want . . .

DIDION: Well, he was always trying . . .

GROSS: . . . for the survivor?

DIDION: He was always trying to have that conversation with me, and I would in many ways not have it because I thought it was—because I see now it was threatening to me, and I was afraid of it. But what I thought then was that it was just dwelling on things that weren't going to happen or dwelling on things that we couldn't help or—you know. And so—I mean, he gave me any number of—he was always giving me also—because he did have this streak of Irish morbidity—he was always talking about his funeral and giving me new lists of people who could or could not speak, as he was kind of volatile in his likes and dislikes. And of course, I—at the key moment, I couldn't find any of those lists. I mean, they'd been changed so often anyway that it made no—that it would have made no difference.

GROSS: I want to quote something you write in your memoir, *The Year of Magical Thinking.* You write,

> Marriage is memory, marriage is time . . . Marriage is not only time: it is also, paradoxically, the denial of time. For forty years I saw myself through John's eyes. I did not age. This year for the first time since I was twenty-nine I saw myself through the eyes of others. This year for the first time since I was twenty-nine I realized that my image of myself was of someone significantly younger.

DIDION: Right.

GROSS: As writers, you both worked at home, and you were with each other just about all the time. Did you have a sense of who you were outside of the marriage, who you were as a single Joan Didion as opposed to a Joan Didion and John Gregory Dunne as a unit?

DIDION: Not really, no. The family was my unit, was kind of the way I—that was actually the way I wanted it. So no, I— so it was kind of necessary to find my—you know, to re-find myself. I hadn't particularly liked being single.

GROSS: When you were younger you mean?

DIDION: When I was younger.

GROSS: Were there parts of yourself that you kind of relied on him to do? I mean—you know what I mean?

DIDION: All parts. I mean, people often say that he'd finish sentences for me. Well, he did, which meant that I—I mean, I just relied on him. He was between me and the world. He not only answered the telephone; he finished my sentences. He was the baffle between me and the world at large.

GROSS: So how are you negotiating the world now, now that there isn't that baffle?

DIDION: Well, it's like everything else; you learn to do it. I mean, I remember when I stopped smoking, it was very hard to know how to arrange me, to walk around as an adult person, because I had been smoking at that point since I was fifteen, and this is kind of like relearning all—I mean, you kind of just learn new—it's not difficult. It's just sort of lonely to—I mean, it's sort of a bleak thing to do.

GROSS: Are you comfortable being alone?

DIDION: Yeah. I've always been comfortable being alone. So that is not the problem. Basically one thing that everybody who has been in a close marriage and who is—what everyone thinks when his or her spouse dies is it's the way in which you are struck at every moment with something you need to tell him.

GROSS: Right. In that passage that I just quoted, you say that this was the first time—after his death—was the first time that you realized your image of yourself was of someone significantly younger.

DIDION: Right.

GROSS: I think I know exactly what you mean, but I'm going to ask you to elaborate on that anyway.

DIDION: Well, you know, I mean, I just—John saw me as, in a sense—I mean, he didn't really, but he gave the impression of seeing me as I'd been when he met me or when he married me. And basically it seemed to me that we were always—we were still grappling with the same questions and problems that we had been dealing with as very—you know, when we were twenty-nine, thirty, thirty-one. We were still doing the same things. We were still worried about the same things. We were the same people. So I didn't really think of myself as getting older.

GROSS: Your husband died five days after your daughter had been hospitalized for pneumonia. By the time he died, she had also gone into septic shock . . .

DIDION: Right.

GROSS: . . . basically a blood infection.

DIDION: Yeah.

GROSS: So you're dealing—you had just gotten back from the hospital, visiting her, when he died.

DIDION: Well, we had been seeing her in the hospital, yeah. It could not be described as a visit, really, because she was unconscious.

GROSS: She was in a coma.

DIDION: She was in an induced coma because she was on a ventilator, and they kept her under heavy sedation so that she wouldn't tear out the ventilator, which people tend to do when they find something going down their throats.

GROSS: So you had to figure out how to tell her when she came out of the coma.

DIDION: Right.

GROSS: You had to figure out how to tell her that her father had died. Why did you want to even bring that up while she was . . .

DIDION: Well, she was going to . . .

GROSS: . . . so fragile? Yeah.

DIDION: Well, I didn't want to bring it up. It was the last thing I wanted to bring up, but the minute she saw me, I knew she would ask where her father was. And so I wasn't planning to see her. I thought that it would be good if—at the time when they lifted the sedation, if her husband were there and she would be kind of in and out for a few days, the doctors said. And so she would absorb that her husband was there, and then she would probably go back to sleep, and she would be focused on—they'd only been married five months, and so she would kind of focus on him and on their life together. And it wouldn't in the natural course of things, maybe, occur to her to ask how her father was. But if she saw me, that's the first question she would ask: "Where is Daddy?"

So I hadn't planned to be there. I'd planned to stay away for the—I was in the hospital. I was out in the corridor when they lifted the sedation. And, unfortunately, the nurse told her that I was out there, so then she wanted me to come in. So I did, and I told her because of the first thing she asked me: "Where's Daddy?" So I told her, but because she was so sedated still—I mean, it took several days for the sedation really to lift—she didn't remember it that night when I came back.

GROSS: And you had to tell her again.

DIDION: I had to tell her again, 'cause she asked how he was, and I said—and so I explained that—I said, "You remember today I told you, et cetera?" And I'd kind of emphasized the long history of cardiac, and she had—what she said to me was—when I said, "You remember this morning, I told you he'd had a heart attack?" And she said, "Yes, but how is he now?" She had absorbed the problem, but she hadn't absorbed what happened—the outcome.

GROSS: Your daughter got out of the hospital. She had several major setbacks, but at the end of your memoir you think that she's on the verge of really resuming her life. In August, after you'd finished your memoir, your daughter died, and this was about a year and a half after your husband's death. She was thirty-nine.

DIDION: Right. Right.

GROSS: You had just examined your grief over your husband so thoroughly in writing about it, and then it was time to grieve again. Now with your husband, you understood the magical thinking that you were going through, this impossible belief that somehow he was going to come back, so you shouldn't even, like, throw out his clothes because he'd need them if he came back. Having examined your grief so carefully, were there little tricks that one plays on oneself when one's grieving that you couldn't even do anymore because you'd seen through it by writing your memoir?

DIDION: Well, you see, I haven't really started grieving yet.

GROSS: For your daughter?

DIDION: Right. I think I'm still in the shock phase. And right after John died, I had—there was a long period before I was able to grieve because I was focused entirely on getting Quintana well. And I think that was—in a way it was very good because by the time I was able to deal with it, I was dealing with it not quite as a crazy person, which I certainly would have been at the beginning.

GROSS: You had to deal with one thing that is a very, I think, peculiar thing to have to deal with when you're grieving for the loss of a child. You had to figure out—well, did you have to rewrite or update your book? You know, your memoir had just been sent in. Your daughter . . .

DIDION: It never crossed my mind.

GROSS: It never crossed your mind to rewrite it?

DIDION: It never crossed my mind. No. It was finished.

GROSS: Why not?

DIDION: Well, it was about a certain period of time after John died, and that period was over. I mean, if I were to do something about Quintana, which I have no thought of doing, it would be a different book. It would be a different—it would be a thing of its own. It wouldn't be about a marriage. This book is about a marriage.

GROSS: Things like death and other tragedies tend to test people's faith if they have it, or get them to immerse themselves deeper into faith, or affirm their lack of faith, or have them change from one point of view to another. I don't know if you've ever had any faith, and if at all the deaths of your daughter and husband affected that.

DIDION: No, the deaths of my daughter and husband did not affect it. Whether I've had any faith is—I have a kind of faith, but it's not a conventional kind of faith. And as I said someplace in the book, that basically I believe in geology and in the Episcopal litany, but as a—I believe in certain symbols, but I don't believe in them as literal truth. I believe in a poetic truth.

GROSS: Do you have any—what is death to you? I mean, when you think about death, do you think of there being some kind of afterlife, or just, you know, like a void or a soul or . . .

DIDION: No, I don't believe in afterlife. Well, you know, what is death to me? Death is ashes to ashes, dust to dust. Yeah. There's a continuum which—there's a continuum of things but it's not—I don't believe in a—I remember somebody once saying to me, the manager of a motel where I was staying—I was doing a piece in Oregon—and this motel manager had just come back from a funeral, and he said it was the most depressing thing he'd ever been to. He said, "It was the coldest funeral I've ever been to. It was an Episcopalian funeral. Have you ever been to one?" I said, "Yes, I have." And he said, "They are so cold." And I said, "How to you mean?" And he said, "If you can't believe you're going to heaven in your own body, and on a first-name basis with everybody in your family, what's the point of dying?" And I loved this. I mean, it just—it was so far from any kind of church I knew, you know? I mean, the whole question, what's the point of dying? Well, yes, what is the point? It was—there was a kind of madness about it. I mean, that's the faith I don't have.

GROSS: Do you ever wish you did? Do you ever envy, like that man, for instance, who has that kind of faith, that, you know, he's going to die and be reunited in heaven . . .

DIDION: And that the . . . [*unintelligible*].

GROSS: . . . in his clothes and his body—yeah.

DIDION: Yeah. Sure. That would be, I suppose, very comforting, but I—there's no possible way I could have it.

GROSS: Are you feeling overwhelmed now by the fragility of life, having lost your daughter and husband?

DIDION: Well, I certainly felt it after John died. Yes, I am a little on the wary side. A friend was having sort of a minor procedure today, and I was very anxious. I found myself being far more anxious about it than I might normally have been.

GROSS: Are you any more or less worried about your own death now?

DIDION: No, I'm not worried about my own death. I think I'm less worried.

GROSS: Why?

DIDION: One of the things that worries us about dying always is we're afraid we're leaving people behind, and they won't be able to take care of themselves; we have to take care of them. But in fact, you see, I'm not leaving anybody behind. This is an area we shouldn't get into, I think.

GROSS: That's fine. That's fine. Do you want another minute before we talk more?

DIDION: Yes.

GROSS: Yeah.

[We're listening to the conversation I recorded yesterday with Joan Didion. While we paused for a moment, my producer told me that this year's National Book Award nominees had just been announced. Then we continued the interview.]

While you were just collecting your thoughts for a second, my producer just came in and said—and I don't know if you know this or not, but it just came across the wire—that your memoir was nominated for a National Book Award.

DIDION: Really?

GROSS: Yeah.

DIDION: Oh, well, great.

GROSS: So I guess let me be the first to congratulate you.

DIDION: Well, thank you. Thank you.

GROSS: What a weird time for you to . . .

DIDION: Yeah.

GROSS: I mean, the book, I understand, is like flying off the shelves. It's nominated for a National Book Award, and it's about the worst thing that's ever happened to you in your life.

DIDION: Yeah. It's sort of—there is a mixed feeling about it, I mean, in my mind. On the other hand, it would make John happy.

GROSS: Oh, yeah.

DIDION: I think he'd be very gratified.

GROSS: I know that among other things, your book will be read by a lot of people who have, you know, gone through their own grief. What were some of the things that you've read that you found helpful? You know, one of the things that really surprised me actually in your book is that you single out Emily Post.

DIDION: Emily . . .

GROSS: You went back to those—yeah.

DIDION: Emily Post was fantastic on the whole subject of death and how to handle people who are grieving. I mean, she's so practical. She simply dealt with what happens to them physiologically. They're cold—they're going to be cold. They're going to need—their digestion is going to stop. Everything stops. Everything in your body just stops when you're going through something like that. And so she suggested ways to get them back to life. Have them sit by the fire. The room should be sunny. They can be served small amounts of toast and—or something they like, but not much because they will reject it, you can sort of—if you just hand them something when they come home from the funeral, you will find that they eat it, but if you ask them, they will say no.

Actually, I got a—well, Knopf got a letter from one of her descendants who now edits the cookbook or the etiquette book, and she pointed out that this, the 1922 edition, which is the edition that I was reading, had been written not long after the death of Emily Post's son. Almost everybody in that period had somebody die close to them. I mean, we were dealing with the aftermath of the 1918 flu epidemic. People died of infections. I mean, death was really in every household. It was a much more commonly acknowledged thing than it is now. I mean, now when it happens in hospitals, we tend to think of it as the province of doctors, where at that time, anybody—everybody knew somebody who was in mourning.

GROSS: Before we say goodbye, I'm just wondering. I felt a little uncomfortable during this interview only because, you know, the memoir is such a fine book, and I think your losses are still so recent, I feel awkward talking with you about them.

I imagine it must be awkward for you to be talking about it to people you don't know, like me, and to our listeners. At the same time, I understand that there might be some comfort in that because one of the things you've always been as a writer is a reporter, not a reporter in the conventional sense but as a more poetic form of reporter who observes the things around you in the world and reports on that for the rest of us. Do you feel like that's what you're doing now?

DIDION: Well, I think—I mean, I had a very definite sense of reporting when I was doing this book, and I don't mean reporting, doing the research, and there was a certain amount of research I did—I mean, I did some reading about grief and I read all the psychiatrists—but I mean a sense of reporting from a different—from a state that not everybody had yet entered—I mean, that some people had but hadn't reported back. I thought there might be some use in reporting back, in sending a dispatch, in filing.

GROSS: Well, Joan Didion, I'm glad that you decided to actually write this book, and I want to thank you very much for talking with us.

DIDION: Thank you.

THE ART OF NONFICTION NO. 1

INTERVIEW BY HILTON ALS
THE PARIS REVIEW
SPRING 2006

The last time this magazine spoke with Joan Didion, in August of 1977, she was living in California and had just published her third novel, *A Book of Common Prayer*. Didion was forty-two years old and well-known not only for her fiction but also for her work in magazines—reviews, reportage, and essays—some of which had been collected in *Slouching Towards Bethlehem* (1968). In addition, Didion and her husband, John Gregory Dunne (who was himself the subject of a *Paris Review* interview in 1996), had written a number of screenplays together, including *The Panic in Needle Park* (1971); an adaptation of her second novel, *Play It as It Lays* (1972); and *A Star Is Born* (1976). When Didion's first interview appeared in these pages in 1978, she was intent on exploring her gift for fiction and nonfiction. Since then, her breadth and craft as a writer have only grown deeper with each project.

Joan Didion was born in Sacramento, and both her parents, too, were native Californians. She studied English at Berkeley, and in 1956, after graduating, she won an essay contest sponsored by *Vogue* and moved to New York City to join the magazine's editorial staff. While at *Vogue*, she wrote fashion copy, as well as book and movie reviews. She also became a frequent contributor to the *National Review*, among other publications. In 1963, Didion published her first novel, *Run*,

River. The next year she married Dunne, and soon afterwards, they moved to Los Angeles. There, in 1965, they adopted their only child, Quintana Roo.

In 1973, Didion began writing for *The New York Review of Books*, where she has remained a regular contributor. While she has continued to write novels in recent decades—*Democracy* (1984) and *The Last Thing He Wanted* (1996)—she has increasingly explored different forms of nonfiction: critical essay, political reportage, memoir. In 1979, she published a second collection of her magazine work, *The White Album*, which was followed by *Salvador* (1983), *Miami* (1987), *After Henry* (1992), *Political Fictions* (2001), and *Where I Was From* (2003). In the spring of 2005, Didion was awarded a Gold Medal from the American Academy of Arts and Letters.

In December of 2003, shortly before their fortieth anniversary, Didion's husband died. Last fall, she published *The Year of Magical Thinking*, a book-length meditation on grief and memory. It became a bestseller, and won the National Book Award for nonfiction; Didion is now adapting the book for the stage as a monologue. Two months before the book's publication, Didion's thirty-nine-year-old daughter died after a long illness.

Our conversation took place over the course of two afternoons in the Manhattan apartment Didion shared with her husband. On the walls of the spacious flat, one could see many photographs of Didion, Dunne, and their daughter. Daylight flooded the book-filled parlor. "When we got the place, we assumed the sun went all through the apartment. It doesn't," Didion said, laughing. Her laughter was the additional punctuation to her precise speech.

HILTON ALS: By now you've written at least as much nonfiction as you have fiction. How would you describe the difference between writing the one or the other?

JOAN DIDION: Writing fiction is for me a fraught business, an occasion of daily dread for at least the first half of the novel, and sometimes all the way through. The work process is totally different from writing nonfiction. You have to sit down every day and make it up. You have no notes—or sometimes you do, I made extensive notes for *A Book of Common Prayer*—but the notes give you only the background, not the novel itself. In nonfiction the notes give you the piece. Writing nonfiction is more like sculpture, a matter of shaping the research into the finished thing. Novels are like paintings, specifically watercolors. Every stroke you put down you have to go with. Of course you can rewrite, but the original strokes are still there in the texture of the thing.

ALS: Do you do a lot of rewriting?

DIDION: When I'm working on a book, I constantly retype my own sentences. Every day I go back to page one and just retype what I have. It gets me into a rhythm. Once I get over maybe a hundred pages, I won't go back to page one, but I might go back to page fifty-five, or twenty, even. But then every once in a while I feel the need to go to page one again and start rewriting. At the end of the day, I mark up the pages I've done—pages or page—all the way back to page one. I mark them up so that I can retype them in the morning. It gets me past that blank terror.

ALS: Did you do that sort of retyping for *The Year of Magical Thinking*?

DIDION: I did. It was especially important with this book because so much of it depended on echo. I wrote it in three months, but I marked it up every night.

ALS: The book moves quickly. Did you think about how your readers would read it?

DIDION: Of course, you always think about how it will be read. I always aim for a reading in one sitting.

ALS: At what point did you know that the notes you were writing in response to John's death would be a book for publication?

DIDION: John died December 30, 2003. Except for a few lines written a day or so after he died, I didn't begin making the notes that became the book until the following October. After a few days of making notes, I realized that I was thinking about how to structure a book, which was the point at which I realized that I was writing one. This realization in no way changed what I was writing.

ALS: Was it difficult to finish the book? Or were you happy to have your life back—to live with a lower level of self-scrutiny?

DIDION: Yes. It was difficult to finish the book. I didn't want to let John go. I don't really have my life back yet, since Quintana died only on August 26.

ALS: Since you write about yourself, interviewers tend to ask about your personal life; I want to ask you about writing and books. In the past you've written pieces on V. S. Naipaul, Graham Greene, Norman Mailer, and Ernest Hemingway—titanic, controversial iconoclasts whom you tend to defend. Were these the writers you grew up with and wanted to emulate?

DIDION: Hemingway was really early. I probably started reading him when I was just eleven or twelve. There was just something magnetic to me in the arrangement of those sentences. Because they were so simple—or rather they appeared to be so simple, but they weren't.

Something I was looking up the other day, that's been in the back of my mind, is a study done several years ago about young women's writing skills and the incidence of Alzheimer's. As it happens, the subjects were all nuns, because all of these women had been trained in a certain convent. They found that those who wrote simple sentences as young women later had a higher incidence of Alzheimer's, while those who wrote complicated sentences with several clauses had a lower incidence of Alzheimer's. The assumption—which I thought was probably erroneous—was that those who tended to write simple sentences as young women did not have strong memory skills.

ALS: Though you wouldn't classify Hemingway's sentences as simple.

DIDION: No, they're deceptively simple because he always brings a change in.

ALS: Did you think you could write that kind of sentence? Did you want to try?

DIDION: I didn't think that I could do them, but I thought that I could learn—because they felt so natural. I could see how they worked once I started typing them out. That was when I was about fifteen. I would just type those stories. It's a great way to get rhythms into your head.

ALS: Did you read anyone else before Hemingway?

DIDION: No one who attracted me in that way. I had been reading a lot of plays. I had a misguided idea that I wanted to act. The form this took was not acting, however, but reading plays. Sacramento was not a place where you saw a lot of plays. I think the first play I ever saw was the Lunts in the touring company of *O Mistress Mine*. I don't think that that's what inspired me. The Theatre Guild used to do plays on the radio, and I remember being very excited about listening to them. I remember memorizing speeches from *Death of a Salesman* and *The Member of the Wedding* in the period right after the war.

ALS: Which playwrights did you read?

DIDION: I remember at one point going through everything of Eugene O'Neill's. I was struck by the sheer theatricality of his plays. You could see how they worked. I read them all one summer. I had nosebleeds, and for some reason it took all summer to get the appointment to get my nose cauterized. So I just lay still on the porch all day and read Eugene O'Neill. That was all I did. And dab at my face with an ice cube.

ALS: What you really seem to have responded to in these early influences was style—voice and form.

DIDION: Yes, but another writer I read in high school who just knocked me out was Theodore Dreiser. I read *An American Tragedy* all in one weekend and couldn't put it down—I locked myself in my room. Now that was antithetical to every other book I was reading at the time because Dreiser really had no style, but it was powerful.

And one book I totally missed when I first read it was *Moby-Dick*. I reread it when Quintana was assigned it in high school. It was clear that she wasn't going to get through it unless we did little talks about it at dinner. I had not gotten it at all when I read it at her age. I had missed that wild control of language. What I had thought discursive were really these great leaps. The book had just seemed a jumble; I didn't get the control in it.

ALS: After high school you wanted to go to Stanford. Why?

DIDION: It's pretty straightforward—all my friends were going to Stanford.

ALS: But you went to Berkeley and majored in literature. What were you reading there?

DIDION: The people I did the most work on were Henry James and D. H. Lawrence, who I was not high on. He irritated me on almost every level.

ALS: He didn't know anything about women at all.

DIDION: No, nothing. And the writing was so clotted and sentimental. It didn't work for me on any level.

ALS: Was he writing too quickly, do you think?

DIDION: I don't know; I think he just had a clotted and sentimental mind.

ALS: You mentioned reading *Moby-Dick*. Do you do much rereading?

DIDION: I often reread *Victory*, which is maybe my favorite book in the world.

ALS: Conrad? Really? Why?

DIDION: The story is told thirdhand. It's not a story the narrator even heard from someone who experienced it. The narrator seems to have heard it from people he runs into around the Malacca Strait. So there's this fantastic distancing of the narrative, except that when you're in the middle of it, it remains very immediate. It's incredibly skillful. I have never started a novel—I mean except the first, when I was starting a novel just to start a novel—I've never written one without rereading *Victory*. It opens up the possibilities of a novel. It makes it seem worth doing. In the same way, John and I always prepared for writing a movie by watching *The Third Man*. It's perfectly told.

ALS: Conrad was also a huge inspiration for Naipaul, whose work you admire. What drew you to Naipaul?

DIDION: I read the nonfiction first. But the novel that really attracted me—and I still read the beginning of it now and then—is *Guerrillas*. It has that bauxite factory in the opening pages, which just gives you the whole feel of that part of the world. That was a thrilling book to me. The nonfiction had the same effect on me as reading Elizabeth Hardwick—you get the sense that it's possible simply to go through life noticing things and writing them down and that this is OK; it's worth doing. That the seemingly insignificant things that most of us spend our days noticing are really significant, have meaning, and tell us something. Naipaul is a great person to read before you have to do a piece. And Edmund Wilson, his essays for *The American Earthquake*. They have that everyday-traveler-in-the-world aspect, which is the opposite of an authoritative tone.

ALS: Was it as a student at Berkeley that you began to feel that you were a writer?

DIDION: No, it began to feel almost impossible at Berkeley because we were constantly being impressed with the fact that everybody else had done it already and better. It was very daunting to me. I didn't think I could write. It took me a couple of years after I got out of Berkeley before I dared to start writing. That academic mind-set—which was kind of shallow in my case anyway—had begun to fade. Then I did write a novel over a long period of time, *Run, River*. And after that it seemed feasible that maybe I could write another one.

ALS: You had come to New York by then and were working at *Vogue*, while writing at night. Did you see writing that novel as a way of being back in California?

DIDION: Yes, it was a way of not being homesick. But I had a really hard time getting the next book going. I couldn't get past a few notes. It was *Play It as It Lays*, but it wasn't called that—I mean it didn't have a name and it wasn't what it is. For one, it was set in New York. Then, in June of 1964, John and I went to California and I started doing pieces for *The Saturday Evening Post*. We needed the money because neither one of us was working. And during the course of doing these pieces I was out in the world enough that an actual story for this so-called second novel presented itself, and then I started writing it.

ALS: What had you been missing about California? What were you not getting in New York?

DIDION: Rivers. I was living on the East Side, and on the weekend I'd walk over to the Hudson and then I'd walk back to the East River. I kept thinking, "All right, they are rivers, but they aren't California rivers." I really missed California rivers. Also the sun going down in the west. That's one of the big advantages to Columbia-Presbyterian Hospital—you can see the sunset. There's always something missing about late afternoon to me on the East Coast. Late afternoon on the West Coast ends with the sky doing all its brilliant stuff. Here it just gets dark.

The other thing I missed was horizons. I missed that on the West Coast, too, if we weren't living at the beach, but I noticed at some point that practically every painting or lithograph I bought had a horizon in it. Because it's very soothing.

ALS: Why did you decide to come back east in 1988?

DIDION: Part of it was that Quintana was in college here, at Barnard, and part of it was that John was between books and having a hard time getting started on a new one. He felt that it was making him stale to be in one place for a long time. We had been living in Brentwood for ten years, which was longer than we had ever lived in any one place. And I think he just thought it was time to move. I didn't particularly, but we left. Even before moving, we had a little apartment in New York. To justify having it, John felt that we had to spend some periods of time there, which was extremely inconvenient for me. The apartment in New York was not very comfortable, and on arrival you would always have to arrange to get the windows washed and get food in... It was cheaper when we stayed at the Carlyle.

ALS: But when you finally moved to New York, was it a bad move?

DIDION: No, it was fine. It just took me about a year, maybe two years all told. The time spent looking for an apartment, selling the house in California, the actual move, having work done, remembering where I put things when I unpacked— it probably took two years out of my effective working life. Though I feel that it's been the right place to be after John died. I would not have wanted to be in a house in Brentwood Park after he died.

ALS: Why not?

DIDION: For entirely logistical reasons. In New York I didn't need to drive to dinner. There wasn't likely to be a brush fire. I wasn't going to see a snake in the pool.

ALS: You said that you started writing for *The Saturday Evening Post* because you and John were broke. Is that where the idea of working for movies came from—the need for cash?

DIDION: Yes it was. One of the things that had made us go to Los Angeles was we had a nutty idea that we could write for television. We had a bunch of meetings with television executives, and they would explain to us, for example, the principle of *Bonanza*. The principle of *Bonanza* was: break a leg at the Ponderosa. I looked blankly at the executive and he said, "Somebody rides into town, and to make the story work, he's got to break a leg so he's around for two weeks." So we never wrote for *Bonanza*. We did, however, have one story idea picked up by Chrysler Theatre. We were paid a thousand dollars for it.

That was also why we started to write for the movies. We thought of it as a way to buy time. But nobody was asking us to write movies. John and his brother Nick and I took an option on *The Panic in Needle Park* and put it together ourselves. I had read the book by James Mills and it just immediately said movie to me. I think that the three of us each put in a thousand dollars, which was enormous at the time.

ALS: How did you make it work as a collaboration? What were the mechanics?

DIDION: On that one, my memory is that I wrote the treatment, which was just voices. Though whenever I say I did something, or vice versa, the other person would go over it, run it through the typewriter. It was always a back-and-forth thing.

ALS: Did you learn anything about writing from the movie work?

DIDION: Yes. I learned a lot of fictional technique. Before I'd written movies, I never could do big set-piece scenes with a lot of different speakers—when you've got twelve people around a dinner table talking at cross-purposes. I had always been impressed by other people's ability to do that. Anthony Powell comes to mind. I think the first book I did those big scenes in was *A Book of Common Prayer*.

ALS: But screenwriting is very different from prose narrative.

DIDION: It's not writing. You're making notes for the director—for the director more than the actors. Sydney Pollack once told us that every screenwriter should go to the Actors Studio because there was no better way to learn what an actor needed. I'm guilty of not thinking enough about what actors need. I think instead about what the director needs.

ALS: John wrote that Robert De Niro asked you to write a scene in *True Confessions* without a single word of dialogue—the opposite of your treatment for *The Panic in Needle Park*.

DIDION: Yeah, which is great. It's something that every writer understands, but if you turn in a scene like that to a producer, he's going to want to know where the words are.

ALS: At the other end of the writing spectrum, there's *The New York Review of Books* and your editor there, Robert Silvers. In the seventies you wrote for him about Hollywood, Woody Allen, Naipaul, and Patty Hearst. All of those essays were, broadly speaking, book reviews. How did you make the shift to pure reporting for the *Review*?

DIDION: In 1982, John and I were going to San Salvador, and Bob expressed interest in having one or both of us write something about it. After we'd been there a few days, it became clear that I was going to do it rather than John, because John was working on a novel. Then when I started writing it, it got very long. I gave it to Bob, in its full length, and my idea was that he would figure out something to take from it. I didn't hear from him for a long time. So I wasn't expecting much, but then he called and said he was going to run the whole thing, in three parts.

ALS: So he was able to find the through-line of the piece?

DIDION: The through-line in *Salvador* was always pretty clear: I went somewhere, this is what I saw. Very simple, like a travel piece. How Bob edited *Salvador* was by constantly nudging me toward updates on the situation and by pointing out weaker material. When I gave him the text, for example, it had a very weak ending, which was about meeting an American evangelical student on the flight home. In other words it was the travel piece carried to its logical and not very interesting conclusion. The way Bob led me away from this was to suggest not that I cut it (it's still there), but that I follow it—and so ground it—with a return to the political situation.

ALS: How did you decide to write about Miami in 1987?

DIDION: Ever since the Kennedy assassination, I had wanted to do something that took place in that part of the world. I thought it was really interesting that so much of the news in America, especially if you read through the assassination hearings, was coming out of our political relations with the Caribbean and Central and South America. So when we got the little apartment in New York, I thought, "Well that's something useful I can do out of New York: I can fly to Miami."

ALS: Had you spent time down south before that?

DIDION: Yes, in 1970. I had been writing a column for *Life*, but neither *Life* nor I was happy with it. We weren't on the same page. I had a contract, so if I turned something in, they had to pay me. But it was soul-searing to turn things in that didn't run. So after about seven columns, I quit. It was agreed that I would do longer pieces. And I said that I was interested in driving around the Gulf Coast, and somehow that got translated into "The Mind of the White South." I had a theory that if I could understand the South, I would understand something about California, because a lot of the California settlers came from the Border South. So I wanted to look into that. It turned out that what I was actually interested in was the South as a gateway to the Caribbean. I should have known that at the time because my original plan had been to drive all over the Gulf Coast.

We began that trip in New Orleans and spent a week there. New Orleans was fantastic. Then we drove around the Mississippi Coast, and that was fantastic too, but in New Orleans, you get a strong sense of the Caribbean. I used a lot of that week in New Orleans in *Common Prayer*. It was the most interesting place I had been in a long time. It was a week in which everything everybody said was astonishing to me.

ALS: Three years later you started writing for *The New York Review of Books*. Was that daunting? In your essay "Why I Write" you express trepidation about intellectual, or ostensibly intellectual, matters. What freed you up enough to do that work for Bob?

DIDION: His trust. Nothing else. I couldn't even have imagined it if he hadn't responded. He recognized that it was a learning experience for me. Domestic politics, for example, was something I simply knew nothing about. And I had no interest. But Bob kept pushing me in that direction. He is really good at ascertaining what might interest you at any given moment and then just throwing a bunch of stuff at you that might or might not be related, and letting you go with it.

When I went to the political conventions in 1988—it was the first time I'd ever been to a convention—he would fax down to the hotel the front pages of *The New York Times* and *The Washington Post*. Well, you know, if there's anything you can get at a convention it's a newspaper. But he just wanted to make sure.

And then he's meticulous once you turn in a piece, in terms of making you plug in all relevant information so that everything gets covered and defended before the letters come. He spent a lot of time, for example, making sure that I acknowledged all the issues in the Terri Schiavo piece, which had the potential for eliciting strong reactions. He's the person I trust more than anybody.

ALS: Why do you think he pushed you to write about politics?

DIDION: I think he had a sense that I would be outside it enough.

ALS: No insider reporting—you didn't know anyone.

DIDION: I didn't even know their names!

ALS: But now your political writing has a very strong point of view—you take sides. Is that something that usually happens during the reporting process, or during the writing?

DIDION: If I am sufficiently interested in a political situation to write a piece about it, I generally have a point of view, although I don't usually recognize it. Something about a situation will bother me, so I will write a piece to find out what it is that bothers me.

ALS: When you moved into writing about politics, you moved away from the more personal writing you'd been doing. Was that a deliberate departure?

DIDION: Yes, I was bored. For one thing, that kind of writing is limiting. Another reason was that I was getting a very strong response from readers, which was depressing because there was no way for me to reach out and help them back. I didn't want to become Miss Lonelyhearts.

ALS: And the pieces on El Salvador were the first in which politics really drive the narrative.

DIDION: Actually it was a novel, *Common Prayer*. We had gone to a film festival in Cartagena and I got sick there, some kind of salmonella. We left Cartagena and went to Bogotá, and then we came back to Los Angeles and I was sick for about four months. I started doing a lot of reading about South America, where I'd never been. There's a passage by Christopher Isherwood in a book of his called

The Condor and the Cows, in which he describes arriving in Venezuela and being astonished to think that it had been down there every day of his life. That was the way that I felt about South America. Then later I started reading a lot about Central America because it was becoming clear to me that my novel had to take place in a rather small country. So that was when I started thinking more politically.

ALS: But it still didn't push you into an interest in domestic politics.

DIDION: I didn't get the connection. I don't know why I didn't get the connection, since I wasn't interested in the politics of these countries per se, but rather in how American foreign policy affected them. And the extent to which we are involved abroad is entirely driven by our own domestic politics. So I don't know why I didn't get that.

I started to get this in *Salvador*, but not fully until *Miami*. Our policy with Cuba and with exiles has been totally driven by domestic politics. It still is. But it was very hard for me to understand the process of domestic politics. I could get the overall picture, but the actual words people said were almost unintelligible to me.

ALS: How did it become clearer?

DIDION: I realized that the words didn't have any actual meaning, that they described a negotiation more than they described an idea. But then you begin to see that the lack of specificity is specific in itself, that it is an obscuring device.

ALS: Did it help you when you were working on *Salvador* and *Miami* to talk to the political figures you were writing about?

DIDION: In those cases it did. Though I didn't talk to a lot of American politicians. I remember talking to the then-president of El Salvador, who was astounding. We were talking about a new land reform law and I explained that I couldn't quite understand what was being said about it. We were discussing a provision—Provision 207—that seemed to me to say that landowners could arrange their affairs so as to be unaffected by the reform.

He said, 207 always applied only to 1979. That is what no one understands. I asked, did he mean that 207 applied only to 1979 because no landowner would work against his interests by allowing tenants on his land after 207 took effect? He said, exactly, no one would rent out land under 207. They would have to be crazy to do that.

Well, that was forthright. There are very few politicians who would say exactly.

ALS: Was it helpful to talk with John about your experiences there?

DIDION: It was useful to talk to him about politics because he viscerally understood politics. He grew up in an Irish Catholic family in Hartford, a town where politics was part of what you ate for breakfast. I mean, it didn't take him a long time to understand that nobody was saying anything.

ALS: After *Salvador*, you wrote your next novel, *Democracy*. It seems informed by the reporting you were doing about America's relationship to the world.

DIDION: The fall of Saigon, though it takes place offstage, was the main thing on my mind. Saigon fell while I was teaching at Berkeley in 1975. I couldn't get those images out of my head, and that was the strongest impulse behind *Democracy*. When the book came out, some people wondered why it began with the bomb tests in the Pacific, but I think those bomb tests formed a straight line to pushing the helicopters off the aircraft carriers when we were abandoning Saigon. It was a very clear progression in my mind. Mainly, I wanted to show that you could write a romance and still have the fall of Saigon, or the Iran-Contra affair. It would be hard for me to stay with a novel if I didn't see a very strong personal story at the center of it.

Democracy is really a much more complete version of *Common Prayer*, with basically the same structure. There is a narrator who tries to understand the character who's being talked about and reconstruct the story. I had a very clear picture in my mind of both those women, but I couldn't tell the story without standing way far away. Charlotte, in *Common Prayer*, was somebody who had a very expensive dress with a seam that was coming out. There was a kind of fevered carelessness to her. *Democracy* started out as a comedy, a comic novel. And I think that there is a more even view of life in it. I had a terrible time with it. I don't know why, but it never got easy.

In Brentwood we had a big safe-deposit box to put man-
uscripts in if we left town during fire season. It was such a big
box that we never bothered to clean it out. When we were
moving, in 1988, and I had to go through the box, I found
I don't know how many different versions of the first ninety
pages of *Democracy*, with different dates on them, written
over several years. I would write ninety pages and not be able
to go any further. I couldn't make the switch. I don't know
how that was solved. Many of those drafts began with Billy
Dillon coming to Amagansett to tell Inez that her father had
shot her sister. It was very hard to get from there to any place.
It didn't work. It was too conventional a narrative. I never hit
the spot where I could sail through. I never got to that point,
even at the very end.

ALS: Was that a first for you?

DIDION: It was a first for a novel. I really did not think I was
going to finish it two nights before I finished it. And when I
did finish it, I had a sense that I was just abandoning it, that
I was just calling it. It was sort of like Vietnam itself—why
don't we say just we've won and leave? I didn't have a real
sense of completion about it.

ALS: Your novels are greatly informed by the travel and reporting you do for your nonfiction. Do you ever do research
specifically for the fiction?

DIDION: *Common Prayer* was researched. We had someone
working for us, Tina Moore, who was a fantastic researcher.

She would go to the UCLA library, and I would say, "Bring me back anything on plantation life in Central America." And she would come back and say, "This is really what you're looking for—you'll love this." And it would not be plantation life in Central America. It would be Ceylon, but it would be fantastic. She had an instinct for what was the same story, and what I was looking for. What I was looking for were rules for living in the tropics. I didn't know that, but that's what I found. In *Democracy* I was more familiar with all the places.

ALS: The last novel you wrote was *The Last Thing He Wanted*. That came out in 1996. Had you been working on it for a long time?

DIDION: No. I started it in the early fall or late summer of 1995, and I finished it at Christmas. It was a novel I had been thinking about writing for a while. I wanted to write a novel about the Iran-Contra affair, and get in all that stuff that was being lost. Basically it's a novel about Miami. I wanted it to be very densely plotted. I noticed that conspiracy was central to understanding that part of the world; everybody was always being set up in some way. The plot was going to be so complicated that I was going to have to write it fast or I wouldn't be able to keep it all in my head. If I forgot one little detail it wouldn't work, and half the readers didn't understand what happened in the end. Many people thought that Elena tried to kill Treat Morrison. "Why did she want to kill him?" they would ask me. But she didn't. Someone else did, and set her up. Apparently I didn't make that clear.

I had begun to lose patience with the conventions of writing. Descriptions went first; in both fiction and nonfiction, I just got impatient with those long paragraphs of description. By which I do not mean—obviously—the single detail that gives you the scene. I'm talking about description as a substitute for thinking. I think you can see me losing my patience as early as *Democracy*. That was why that book was so hard to write.

ALS: After *Democracy* and *Miami*, and before *The Last Thing He Wanted*, there was the nonfiction collection *After Henry*, which strikes me as a way of coming back to New York and trying to understand what the city was.

DIDION: It has that long piece "Sentimental Journeys," about the Central Park jogger, which began with that impulse. We had been in New York a year or two, and I realized that I was living here without engaging the city at all. I might as well have been living in another city, because I didn't understand it, I didn't get it. So I realized that I needed to do some reporting on it. Bob and I decided I would do a series of short reporting pieces on New York, and the first one would be about the jogger. But it wasn't really reporting. It was coming at a situation from a lot of angles. I got so involved in it that, by the time I finished the piece, it was too long. I turned it in and Bob had some comments—many, many comments, which caused it to be even longer because he thought it needed so much additional material, which he was right about. By the time I'd plugged it all in, I'd added another six to eight thousand words. When I finally had finished it, I thought, "That's all I have to do about New York."

ALS: Although it is about the city, "Sentimental Journeys" is really about race and class and money.

DIDION: It seemed to me that the case was treated with a lot of contempt by the people who were handling it.

ALS: How so?

DIDION: The prosecution thought they had the press and popular sentiment on their side. The case became a way of expressing the city's rage at being broke and being in another recession and not having a general comfort level, the sense that there were people sleeping on the streets—which there were. We moved here six months after the '87 stock market crash. Over the next couple of years, its effect on Madison Avenue was staggering. You could not walk down Madison Avenue at eight in the evening without having to avoid stepping on people sleeping in every doorway. There was a German television crew here doing a piece on the jogger, and they wanted to shoot in Harlem, but it was late in the day and they were losing the light. They kept asking me what the closest place was where they could shoot and see poverty. I said, "Try Seventy-Second and Madison." You know where Polo is now? That building was empty and the padlocks were broken and you could see rats scuttling around inside. The landlord had emptied it—I presume because he wanted to get higher rents—and then everything had crashed. There was nothing there. That entire block was a mess.

ALS: So from California you had turned your attention to the third world, and now you were able to recognize New York because of the work you had done in the third world.

DIDION: A lot of what I had seen as New York's sentimentality is derived from the stories the city tells itself to rationalize its class contradictions. I didn't realize that until I started doing the jogger piece. Everything started falling into place on that piece. Bob would send me clips about the trial, but on this one I was on my own, because only I knew where it was going.

ALS: In some of your early essays on California, your subject matter was as distinctively your own as your writing style. In recent decades, though, it's not so much the story but your take on the story that makes your work distinctive.

DIDION: The shift came about as I became more confident that my own take was worth doing. In the beginning, I didn't want to do any stories that anyone else was doing. As time went by, I got more comfortable with that. For example, on the Central Park jogger piece I could not get into the courtroom because I didn't have a police pass. This forced me into another approach, which turned out to be a more interesting one. At least to me.

ALS: Wasn't it around the same time that you were also doing the "Letter from Los Angeles" for Robert Gottlieb at *The New Yorker*?

DIDION: Yes. Though I wasn't doing more than two of those a year. I think they only ran six to eight thousand words, but the idea was to do several things in each letter. I had never done that before, where you just really discuss what people are talking about that week. It was easy to do. It was a totally different tone from the *Review*. I went over those *New Yorker* pieces when I collected them. I probably took out some of *The New Yorker*'s editing, which is just their way of making everything sound a certain way.

ALS: Can you characterize your methods as a reporter?

DIDION: I can't ask anything. Once in a while if I'm forced into it I will conduct an interview, but it's usually pro forma, just to establish my credentials as somebody who's allowed to hang around for a while. It doesn't matter to me what people say to me in the interview because I don't trust it. Sometimes you do interviews where you get a lot. But you don't get them from public figures.

When I was conducting interviews for the piece on Lakewood, it was essential to do interviews because that was the whole point. But these were not public figures. On the one hand, we were discussing what I was ostensibly there doing a piece about, which was the Spur Posse, a group of local high school boys who had been arrested for various infractions. But on the other hand, we were talking, because it was the first thing on everyone's mind, about the defense industry going downhill, which was what the town was about. That was a case in which I did interviewing and listened.

ALS: Did the book about California, *Where I Was From*, grow out of that piece, or had you already been thinking about a book?

DIDION: I had actually started a book about California in the seventies. I had written some of that first part, which is about my family, but I could never go anywhere with it for two reasons. One was that I still hadn't figured out California. The other was that I didn't want to figure out California because whatever I figured out would be different from the California my mother and father had told me about. I didn't want to engage that.

ALS: You felt like you were still their child?

DIDION: I just didn't see any point in engaging it. By the time I did the book they were dead.

ALS: You said earlier that after *The White Album* you were tired of personal writing and didn't want to become Miss Lonelyhearts. You must be getting a larger personal response from readers than ever with *The Year of Magical Thinking*. Is that difficult?

DIDION: I have been getting a very strong emotional response to *Magical Thinking*. But it's not a crazy response; it's not demanding. It's people trying to make sense of a fairly universal experience that most people don't talk about. So this is a case in which I have found myself able to deal with the response directly.

ALS: Do you ever think you might go back to the idea of doing little pieces about New York?

DIDION: I don't know. It is still a possibility, but my basic question about New York was answered for me: it's criminal.

ALS: That was your question?

DIDION: Yes, it's criminal.

ALS: Do you find it stimulating in some way to live here?

DIDION: I find it really comfortable. During the time we lived in California, which lasted twenty-four years, I didn't miss New York after the first year. And after the second year I started to think of New York as sentimental. There were periods when I didn't even come to New York at all. One time I realized that I had been to Hong Kong twice since I had last been to New York. Then we started spending more time in New York. Both John and I were really happy to have been here on 9/11. I can't think of any place else I would have rather been on 9/11, and in the immediate aftermath.

ALS: You could have stayed in Sacramento forever as a novelist, but you started to move out into the worlds of Hollywood and politics.

DIDION: I was never a big fan of people who don't leave home. I don't know why. It just seems part of your duty in life.

ALS: I'm reminded of Charlotte in *A Book of Common Prayer*. She has no conception of the outside world but she wants to be in it.

DIDION: Although a novel takes place in the larger world, there's always some drive in it that is entirely personal—even if you don't know it while you're doing it. I realized some years after *A Book of Common Prayer* was finished that it was about my anticipating Quintana's growing up. I wrote it around 1975, so she would have been nine, but I was already anticipating separation and actually working through that ahead of time. So novels are also about things you're afraid you can't deal with.

ALS: Are you working on one now?

DIDION: No. I haven't felt that I wanted to bury myself for that intense a period.

ALS: You want to be in the world a bit.

DIDION: Yeah. A little bit.

JOAN DIDION'S YELLOW CORVETTE

INTERVIEW BY HARI KUNZRU
SEPTEMBER 2011

In September 2011 I went to visit Joan Didion at her apartment on the Upper East Side. I was there to interview her for a British women's magazine about *Blue Nights*, her recently published memoir. We spoke (among other things) about grief, the aesthetics of failure, California and (at the request of the editor) about her friendship with the Redgrave family. Since most of the interesting stuff didn't make it into the piece, here's the full transcript.

HARI KUNZRU: To say I enjoyed *Blue Nights* seems like the wrong term. I admire it, very much.

JOAN DIDION: Thank you.

KUNZRU: When did you know you were writing that? Was it absolutely continuous with the notes you were taking for *The Year of Magical Thinking*?

DIDION: No. Not at all. I was through *Magical Thinking*. It had been turned into a play. And [I] was trying to think— the play ran for a year or two, and obviously I was going to have to think of something else to write, and I decided I wanted to write about children, attitudes towards having children. And I started writing about children and of course I ended up writing willy-nilly about my own child. At that point I thought it was getting very hard for me to write, and I thought—you don't have to do this, you can give Knopf back their money and not do it. So I thought that for a couple of weeks and then something else occurred to me and I wrote it down, and then I saw it was not totally about children, but about other stuff like getting older and I pushed on.

KUNZRU: When you say you pushed on, I'm interested in— how you begin—how you've begun books in general and this one in particular. You take notes—

DIDION: That one. I didn't have any idea what the book was going to be about so I wasn't really taking notes of any use. Then I was very taken—somehow the phrase "blue nights" occurred to me—and I thought you could call it *Blue Nights*. This sounds crazy. That you start a book because you have thought of two words that make you happy.

KUNZRU: It unfolded from the title.

DIDION: It totally unfolded from the title. And so it doesn't actually go anyplace linear, because it unfolded from the title.

KUNZRU: It seems like it's shaped like memory.

DIDION: It's shaped like memory.

KUNZRU: You have these very precise fragments that you pick away at, you make a circuit around them.

DIDION: And then come back.

KUNZRU: "When we talk about mortality we're talking about our children." I wonder if you could say a little more about what you mean by that.

DIDION: I'm not sure what I mean by it. I actually wrote it down. And I started thinking—it's a banal thought, of course—we're talking about our children because we're talking about fear of our children dying, hostages to fortune. Our children are hostages. It was just a flitting from one angle on a thing to another.

KUNZRU: You talk quite a lot about frailty, which I'd like to come back to later. This notion that—you have a child—

DIDION: And you're never not afraid.

KUNZRU: That's an extraordinarily frightening thought. I haven't got any children yet. I'm thinking about having one. And that's precisely what I most fear.

DIDION: It's terrifying.

KUNZRU: About the process of becoming a parent—

DIDION: It's actually terrifying. A lot of people have that feeling about their dogs. And if you're the kind of person who's going to have that feeling about a dog you're definitely going to have that about a child.

KUNZRU: One of the questions that seems to come up for you when you're trying to understand Quintana's childhood is the environment you raised her in, the film colony. There's the extraordinary story about taking her to see *Nicholas and Alexandra* (1971) and her response is "I think it's going to be a big hit." Did that—you obviously found that striking—you were expecting a direct and emotional response to the movie's story. How did you read that? Was that her protecting herself from feeling something? Did you worry she'd become crass in some way?

DIDION: I don't know what I thought. It wasn't a cause of worry to me. It was just a wonder. Everybody she knew would talk that way. It was striking to me that she'd picked up so much. She was born in '63. She was eight or nine.

KUNZRU: You think about the hotels a lot, about taking her to the Dorchester, the Plaza. But you very strongly reject the notion that it was a privileged childhood.

DIDION: I don't think it was privileged. I felt very strongly that I didn't want people to read this about her and think this is an overprivileged child. I think there was a lot in her life that worked against privilege. She had a rather difficult life in a lot of ways.

KUNZRU: Being adopted?

DIDION: Yes. And not being—the fact that she had picked up a certain ability to get along in the world that she'd been placed down in didn't seem to me to be something that should be held against her. [*laughs*]

KUNZRU: You seem ambivalent about seeing her functioning so smoothly in some of those situations.

DIDION: I was ambivalent about it.

KUNZRU: Was that because you didn't want her to grow up so fast?

DIDION: I didn't want her to grow up at all! I wanted her to be a baby forever.

KUNZRU: So the end point was when you brought her back from the adoption, the scene in the restaurant in Hollywood, where she sat on the table in her bassinet and you felt everything was perfect.

DIDION: Yes.

KUNZRU: Back to this word frailty. You write very movingly about it. But it seems [to] me that throughout your works there's been this anxiety and a sense of dread without an object, it's one of the strongest tones that I get from your writing of the sixties and seventies. I think it [is] what's made you such a good writer about California. There's something very specific to California about that dread—anyway—now the dread has an object. In a way, the worst has come.

DIDION: Right. It's an odd time. It should be kind of a liberating time. It's not. I'm no longer hostage.

KUNZRU: You've faced it.

DIDION: Yes.

KUNZRU: And you're still here.

DIDION: It doesn't seem to work that way.

KUNZRU: How does it work?

DIDION: You still have that floating anxiety.

KUNZRU: And you feel that's transferred itself to—the physical—the skateboarder coming down the street, the taxi?

DIDION: Exactly. My fear for Quintana's safety has transferred itself to fears for my safety.

KUNZRU: You write about how peculiar that is, because sometimes you forget this is the body you're in now, you think of yourself as a younger person. I read an old interview with you this morning, from when you were living in California ["Joan

Didion: Staking Out California" by Michiko Kakutani, in *Joan Didion: Essays and Conversations*] which said that the 1969 yellow Corvette Stingray Maria drives in *Play It as It Lays* was actually your car.

DIDION: It was my car.

KUNZRU: Do you still feel connected to that woman? The woman who drove along the coast road to Malibu in a yellow Corvette Stingray?

DIDION: No. At some point in the past year I think I twigged to the fact that I was no longer the woman in the yellow Corvette. Very recently. It wasn't five years ago.

KUNZRU: When you said you "twigged to that," was that a moving on, a sense of loss—

DIDION: Actually, when John died, for the first time I thought—for the first time I realized how old I was, because I'd always thought of myself—when John was alive I saw myself through his eyes and he saw me as how old I was when we got married—and so when he died I kind of looked at myself in a different way. And this has kept on since then. The yellow Corvette. When I gave up the yellow Corvette, I literally gave up on it, I turned it in on a Volvo station wagon. [*laughs*]

KUNZRU: [*laughing*] That's quite an extreme maneuver.

DIDION: The dealer was baffled.

KUNZRU: The Corvette driver would mutate into the Volvo driver. Was that because you were leaving California?

DIDION: No, we had just moved in from Malibu into Brentwood. I needed a new car because with the Corvette something was always wrong, but I didn't need a Volvo station wagon. Maybe it was the idea of moving into Brentwood.

KUNZRU: You were really trying to embody that suburban role. So the Corvette was the car you were driving down the foggy road and trying to work out where the turn for your drive was, and where was just a steep cliff.

DIDION: Yes.

KUNZRU: There are many sudden turns in the book but one I liked—one you got me with—was you write this quite sentimental passage about objects that have memories for you, end the chapter and then announce at the beginning of the next chapter that you "no longer value mementos in that way." That was very startling. And yet we're here in your apartment, surrounded by your things. Your books and photographs. At one point in the book, you're quite resentful of—

DIDION: Things.

KUNZRU: I half expected to find you in some spare, empty space, having done some kind of radical clean out.

DIDION: That was the moment when I thought of moving into Annie Leibovitz's apartment. [Before the interview we'd talked about London Terrace and the apartment Leibovitz and Sontag had shared. She'd seen it when Leibovitz was moving out to her famously disastrous town house. She liked the emptiness of it.]

KUNZRU: So does that mean you've come to terms with objects?

DIDION: I haven't come to terms with them. I don't know what to do with them. There's no resolution to it. I don't want to just throw them out.

KUNZRU: You can't take it all to Housing Works.

DIDION: No. I guess. Some of them wouldn't be any use to Housing Works. The physical act of cleaning out my stuff seems to be beyond me.

KUNZRU: It takes people in different ways, doesn't it? Some people seem to need to have stuff bagged and out the door before they can process anything.

DIDION: When my mother died—my mother died in Monterey. My brother had a house in Pebble Beach so he was there. I knew immediately, because mother had secretly told me, when she died she wanted to make sure he didn't put everything into a dumpster and get rid of it. She wanted certain things to go to certain children, grandchildren, nephews; she wanted me to take care of that. And so I endeavored to do that. I flew out to California, I insisted to my brother that we were going to do this, we were going to divide up her furniture and so on, so he was so unwilling to do this that I ended up sending most of the stuff to this apartment. I'd sent everything that was claimed to that child, and the rest of it stayed here. It's still here. I don't want it.

KUNZRU: But the filing system has broken down, the processing system.

DIDION: Yes.

KUNZRU: You wrote about Natasha Richardson, and you're friends with Vanessa Redgrave. Do you find any value in comparing your grief to the grief of a friend?

DIDION: Vanessa and I became very close during the time we did the play. Actually we'd been weirdly close before because I was a friend of Tony [Richardson]'s. And so I was very fond of her. And then we became very close during the time when we were doing the play. Well, she was doing the play. I wasn't.

KUNZRU: You were drinking cocktails in the vicinity of the play, from your account.

DIDION: Yes [*laughs*] and when Natasha died, we did talk. Obviously we did talk a lot about that. I'm not sure—there's no comfort in talking.

KUNZRU: Not in community?

DIDION: No, I don't think so.

KUNZRU: People do go to groups don't they, to talk. It's never specially been an impulse of mine.

DIDION: It's not mine. I've never done that. Vanessa was a comfort to me, just the fact that she was there.

KUNZRU: She has an extraordinary presence. I knew her brother a bit.

DIDION: Corin.

KUNZRU: Yes. I met her at a stage reading a group of us were doing for Corin [a protest against extralegal detentions in Guantanamo Bay]. She was this—whirlwind of a woman—I think she was particularly distracted when I met her, she had a million things on her mind—she carries her own concerns into the room.

DIDION: Entirely, entirely.

KUNZRU: I found it easiest just to sort of surrender to the atmosphere that she had decided to create.

DIDION: She did *Magical Thinking* not only at the Booth in New York, but at the National Theatre in London. When she was going to do it at the National Theatre she asked me to come over for a week of rehearsals. So the day I arrived in the rehearsal room, I walked into the rehearsal room and the first thing I know is, to act out her pleasure at my arrival she'd thrown her bag at me. Suddenly I realized there was blood running down my leg. I spent the rest of the week making daily visits to the National Health nurse. [*laughs*]

KUNZRU: She damaged you with her extrovert gesture. Was she mortified, or did she not notice?

DIDION: I never told her why I was going to the nurse's office.

KUNZRU: I was very struck by the passage when you reproduce a note you'd taken for a piece of fiction with *x's* marking various placeholders and demonstrate that ease with which you were—in a way—able to fill in those blanks in response to—you say you thought of it as listening to music. And you say that's now gone. That facility. When did that change for you? How is writing now?

DIDION: I think it changed when I was writing this book. I'm not saying it had anything to do with the particular book. Something happened—the ease of my relationship with language disappeared. Now, what that is I have no idea.

KUNZRU: Is it just ease in producing words, and not having them mean too much?

DIDION: Ease in producing words. But they did mean

something. Now, in point of fact when I mention this to certain people, they will say to me—they name a date ten years before when I was making the same complaint that I'd lost my relationship with language, and this may be so. But I feel it now.

KUNZRU: You write that for a while you encouraged that tendency in yourself, because you saw it as a new directness. And directness seems to be an important quality for you in prose.

DIDION: Yes.

KUNZRU: And then you—you decided this wasn't the case at all. You write "I see it now as frailty." What do you mean by frailty? The end of this facility?

DIDION: That it's a failure. As opposed to a technique.

KUNZRU: What kind of a failure?

DIDION: Specifically the failure to have a fluid relationship with language. Or with my means of support.

KUNZRU: And yet, you've written a book that seems stylistically continuous with your previous work. I can tell it's you writing. I don't have a—maybe it's more boiled down, more—

DIDION: It feels very different to me.

KUNZRU: It's the hardest question to answer. How? What if it's not necessarily apparent to the reader, this trace of the difficulty you had making it? [*a long pause*]

For example, could you ever see yourself writing fiction again?

DIDION: Fiction has seemed impossible since I finished *The Last Thing He Wanted* (1996), a book which I had intended to be totally plot-orientated. I'd wanted to do a very densely plotted novel. And I did. It was so densely plotted that I had to—I think I wrote it in ten weeks or something because if you stopped for even a minute you'd forget the plot. I was working—somebody wanted me to make a movie of it, and I was roughing out a draft of a screenplay of it—and even I couldn't remember the plot. I couldn't keep it straight. So it seemed to me that another novel was not the way to go.

KUNZRU: That "plottiness" feels irrelevant, distant now? You prefer the idea of making structures that reflect something more immediate about your experience?

DIDION: It feels like not the right thing to be doing.

KUNZRU: *California v. New York*. You agonized about giving up your California driver's license.

DIDION: Got rid of it. I had to. My birthday came and I had to renew my license and I couldn't get to California. I'd already renewed it enough times by mail. I had to show up. And so I took my California driver's license down to Thirty-Fourth Street and turned it in. I'm a New York driver.

KUNZRU: Do you still have a lot of friends and connections in LA?

DIDION: Yes.

KUNZRU: Do you spend a lot of time there?

DIDION: No I don't. I haven't spent a lot of time there since Quintana was in the hospital.

KUNZRU: And your New York life? Do you see a lot of people at the moment?

DIDION: I see far too many.

KUNZRU: There's a writer—I think you might know her—called Meghan O'Rourke.

DIDION: Oh yes.

KUNZRU: She wrote a memoir about losing her mother [*The Long Goodbye* (2011)]. It was one thing for her to put it down on paper. She did it very soon. And what she found was the business of talking about it, and touring, and doing interviews like this—she found that awful. She found it difficult in a way she wasn't expecting. And I read somewhere that after *Year of Magical Thinking* you did quite a substantial book tour and that you found it therapeutic.

DIDION: I think I did on some level. It was almost immediately after Quintana died. Obviously the trip had been planned long before she was even in the hospital. But it did not cross my mind to cancel it because I simply didn't know what I would do if—I mean, I was never in my whole life going to stop grieving for Quintana. It wasn't a question—it was a question of are you going to live for the rest of your life. Get on a plane and live.

KUNZRU: Distraction is sometimes a good thing, but how was it taking questions from audiences? You must have had people standing up in audiences telling you their stories.

DIDION: They did. Actually it was—because they were interested in telling me their stories rather than hearing about mine, it was kind of great. [*laughs*] I could just lie back. I was a witness to their stories. It was a role I found very comforting.

KUNZRU: In a way, that's the kind of work you've done throughout your career.

DIDION: Listening.

KUNZRU: This is from *The White Album*: "You are getting a woman who somewhere along the line misplaced whatever slight faith she ever had in the social contract, in the meliorative principle . . . I have trouble maintaining the basic notion that keeping promises matters in a world where everything I was taught seems beside the point." That was, I suppose, written partly about the social upheavals of the sixties, but it also seems—do you feel that the way it's worked out—with the loss of your husband and daughter—do you feel that promises have been broken in some way?

DIDION: The loss of my husband was not like the loss of Quintana because it was perfectly predictable. I didn't predict it—but—he was of a certain age, he had heart trouble, this was an acknowledged—even by me—I knew he had heart trouble. It wasn't a secret. He was always having something done to his heart. Anyone else could have figured out in a flash that he'd die from it. But it came as a surprise to me. That was my fault. [*laughs*]

KUNZRU: A failure of imagination.

DIDION: Yes. But Quintana's death was out of the blue.

KUNZRU: Unjust?

DIDION: Unfair. I wouldn't say unfair. Nothing's fair. But it was an unbalanced death.

KUNZRU: And for somebody who had a skeptical relationship with—conventional ideas about the meaning of life—certainly from that passage—that's somebody who's having a hard time working out what it's worth caring about—presumably that feeling's only been augmented by what's happened to you. I mean, is it writing that's providing a center?

DIDION: I haven't got a center. I don't know where my center is. I don't know where I'm going to find it. Once in a while I'll wake up in the middle of the night and think well—I'll have some flash of something that looks like a center, but it doesn't signal—it's a mirage.

KUNZRU: I have one personal question. I'm writing filmscripts with my fiancée, Katie Kitamura, also a novelist, and we've both read you and your husband on the subject, and I wonder if you could say anything about how that partnership worked for you. Are you writing scenes together, or—

DIDION: Here's what we did. We'd work on different parts of the screenplay together. If he started it, I'd usually follow and rewrite. If I started it, he would rewrite.

KUNZRU: One to pioneer—

DIDION: Really only one person can make up the plot. You can't really just sit there and talk out a plot. One person can sit there and come up with the characters. Then the other person can polish that and work out the details. It was whoever was free to start it. The other person would come up behind. Who started it really depended on who didn't have another commitment.

AN INTERVIEW WITH JOAN DIDION

INTERVIEW BY SHEILA HETI
THE BELIEVER
FEBRUARY 1, 2012

One Thursday at noon in December 2011, I spoke to Joan Didion over the phone. She was in a hotel in Washington. The woman at the front desk asked, "Who do you want? Bibion? *B* as in *boy*?" I replied, "No, *d* as in *dog*," feeling weird and a little hostile. "*D* as in *dog*, *i*, *d* as in *dog*, *i*, *o*, *n*." I did not like having to put *dog* in Joan Didion's name. And I did not want to speak to Joan Bibion.

Knopf had given us half an hour to talk. Didion was on book tour for her latest work, the memoir *Blue Nights*. She would be appearing at a bookstore later that day.

I imagined her sitting on the edge of a neatly made bed. I imagined that after we hung up, she would move things about the room, then open the door to another reporter. Or perhaps she would have time to stroll around Washington, take a few hours for herself.

I had been reading only her for the past few weeks: her novels; her essays, collected in *We Tell Ourselves Stories in Order to Live*; *Blue Nights*, written in the wake of her daughter's death from an influenza gone awry, a book about aging and loss and being a mother; and her previous book, the bestselling *The Year of Magical Thinking*, which was about the death of her husband, the writer John

Gregory Dunne. That book returned Joan Didion to the center of America's conversation about itself, a place she has spent serious time since the 1960s, when she first began publishing.

She was born in 1934, and has written like no other about California (where her family lived for generations), and like no other about the profound changes in America in the sixties and seventies, and about political campaigns, and about being a human. In her famous essay "On Self-Respect" she says:

> If we do not respect ourselves, we are on the one hand forced to despise those who have so few resources as to consort with us, so little perception as to remain blind to our fatal weaknesses. On the other, we are peculiarly in thrall to everyone we see, curiously determined to live out—since our self-image is untenable—their false notions of us . . . We play roles doomed to failure before they are begun, each defeat generating fresh despair at the urgency of divining and meeting the next demand made upon us.

I quote this only to say that I felt like I was talking to a person not in anyone's thrall, not living out anyone's false notion of her. There was no pose. Her voice was tremendously sensitive—the tiniest inflections seemed to carry a depth of feeling and perception, and a commitment to neither exaggerate nor underplay nor bend the truth to the right or the left; a rigorous person, yet somehow entirely at ease.

I. PERFORMING

SHEILA HETI: I want to start with something you said in *The Paris Review.* When you were a little girl you wanted to be an actress, not a writer?

JOAN DIDION: Right.

HETI: But you said it's OK, because writing is in some ways a performance. When you're writing, are you performing a character?

DIDION: You're not even a character. You're doing a performance. Somehow writing has always seemed to me to have an element of performance.

HETI: What is the nature of that performance? I mean, an actor performs a character—

DIDION: Sometimes an actor performs a character, but sometimes an actor just performs. With writing, I don't think it's performing a character, really, if the character you're performing is yourself. I don't see that as playing a role. It's just appearing in public.

HETI: Appearing in public and sort of saying lines—

DIDION: But not somebody else's lines. Your lines. "Look at me—this is me" is, I think, what you're saying.

HETI: And do you feel like that "me" is a pretty stable thing, or unstable? Is it consistent through one's life as a writer?

DIDION: I think it develops into a fairly stable thing over time. I think it's not at all stable at first. But then you kind of grow into the role you have made for yourself.

HETI: How would you gauge the distance between the role you have made for yourself—

DIDION: —and the real person?

HETI: Yeah.

DIDION: Well, I don't know. The real person becomes the role you have made for yourself.

HETI: And are you performing for yourself or performing for others?

DIDION: Performing for yourself. But also, obviously, other people are involved. I mean, the reader is your audience.

HETI: How much of the work would you say is created in collaboration or in response to an audience?

DIDION: Oh, I think a lot of it. I did a play based on *The Year of Magical Thinking*, and I was struck by the extent to which the audience became part of the play when it was in performance. The audience was very strongly a part of what went on on the stage. And I think that is also true when you're writing.

HETI: But in the case of writing, the reader is more your imagination of the reader.

DIDION: Well, it's not your imagination of the reader—yes, I guess it is your imagination of the reader because the reader isn't physically there the way the audience is in a theater. But it's just as real a collaboration, I think.

HETI: So what does the reader bring to the collaboration?

DIDION: Well, the same thing an audience brings to an actor. I can't imagine writing if I didn't have a reader. Any more than an actor can imagine acting without an audience.

HETI: They're almost born at the same time—writing and the idea of a reader.

DIDION: Yeah, it simply doesn't exist in a vacuum. If you aren't aware of the reader, you're working in a vacuum.

II. BEGINNING TO WRITE

HETI: Do you remember beginning to write?

DIDION: It was as a child. I was four or five, and my mother gave me a big black tablet, because I kept complaining that I was bored. She said, "Then write something. Then you can read it." In fact, I had just learned to read, so this was a thrilling kind of moment. The idea that I could write something—and then read it!

HETI: Have you gotten pleasure from reading your own writing?

DIDION: Over the years, yes. Not always, but sometimes.

HETI: How would you characterize the kind of pleasure one gets from reading one's own writing when it's good?

DIDION: Well, it's just a deep pleasure to read something you've written yourself—if and when you like it. Just as it's not a deep pleasure if you don't like it.

HETI: And do you feel alienated from any particular period of your work?

DIDION: I never felt close to my first novel, because it simply—I didn't know how to do it, I didn't know how to do what I had in mind. I wanted to mix up the time frame in a way that I was not experienced enough to know how to do, so I eventually did what the editor suggested, and forgot trying to mix up the time frame, and did a very conventional narrative. And that was not a good feeling.

HETI: The book wasn't close to your vision?

DIDION: No, it was totally opposite.

III. GETTING THE CONFIDENCE

HETI: You've said in the past that you don't have a strong sense of reality. You've had a lot of criticism about yourself as a reporter, or have conveyed the feeling that it wasn't naturally what you were. Yet that journalism that you did early in your career, and later in your career, is so strong. When you look back at your essays, do you feel like that is somebody who saw reality, or is it something else?

DIDION: I think, I think it's somebody who saw reality. But it's also something else. I don't know. This is a touchy—not touchy, but it's a difficult thing to separate those thoughts out.

HETI: I imagine it would be difficult to write nonfiction, because you have to have such an authority to say, "This is what the world is." How can you really have the authority to say, "I know enough and I've seen enough to be able to conclude things about the world"?

DIDION: Well, you have to just gain that confidence. Which is part of what you do over the course of your whole career. I mean, you become confident that you have—this sounds ridiculous, but you become confident that you have the answer.

HETI: Do you remember the point—

DIDION: —at which you get that confidence?

HETI: Well, for you.

DIDION: For me it probably occurred fairly late, when I started getting feedback from the audience. Feedback in terms of a response. Well, it wasn't fairly late. It was fairly early [*laughs*] when I started getting a response from the audience, otherwise I wouldn't have had the nerve to continue.

HETI: And where would you situate that? Around which book, say?

DIDION: I would say it happened at *Play It as It Lays*. Which was, when? My third book. And I remember my husband saying, when *Play It as It Lays* was about to come out, "This isn't going to—you're never going to—you're never going to—this book isn't going to make it." And I didn't think it was going to make it, either. And suddenly it did make it, in a minor way. And from that time on I had more confidence.

HETI: Why did you both feel like it wasn't going to make it?

DIDION: Because it was my third book and I had not made it until then. And you don't see—I mean, you don't think in terms of suddenly making it. You think you have some stable talent which will show no matter what you're writing, and if it doesn't seem to be getting across to the audience once, you can't imagine that moment when it suddenly will.

HETI: *Play It as It Lays* was fiction, but that confidence translated into other kinds of writing as well.

DIDION: Yeah. What happened was I started doing a lot of reporting that gradually came to get noticed, so I was asked to do other things. Gradually, gradually you gain that confidence. Well, you know. You've been through this.

HETI: Yes, it's gradual. It stuck in my head when your husband said, "It's not going to make it." Did that hurt your feelings to hear that, or was that simply the way—

DIDION: No, it didn't hurt my feelings. It was, I thought, a realistic assessment. Which I certainly agreed with.

HETI: What was the first sign that there was going to be a real response?

DIDION: I don't remember exactly what it was, but suddenly people were talking about this book. Not in a huge way, but in a way that I hadn't experienced before.

HETI: Did it change your relationship to the book? Did it make you feel more separate from it or anything?

DIDION: No, it didn't make me feel more separate from it. It made me feel good. It made me feel closer to it. Closer to it. I was so unhappy writing that book because it was just a very hard book for me to write, and I didn't realize until I finished it how depressed it had made me to write it. Then I finished it and suddenly it was like having something lifted from the top of my head, you know? Suddenly I was a happy person.

HETI: It always happens, for me, that I have a certain attitude toward the world for the time period I'm writing a book—

DIDION: Right. You borrow the mood of the book in some way.

HETI: It's hard to find a book that's safe to write. Because one always goes to dark or difficult places.

DIDION: Exactly. Sometimes you don't want to go there.

HETI: But then where can you go? I mean, it's the only place to go, right?

DIDION: Right.

IV. WOODY ALLEN'S "RELATIONSHIPS"

HETI: In the seventies, you wrote a fascinating article about Woody Allen's movies—including *Annie Hall* and *Manhattan*—which was published in *The New York Review of Books,* where you put *"relationships"* in quotation marks so much—

DIDION: I think because he was always talking about *relation-ships,* quote unquote.

HETI: But how does it come out of the quotation marks, or how does it get into the quotation marks? Reading the essay, I got the feeling you were saying that the idea of a relationship is something that the culture invented.

DIDION: It's not something that the culture invented. It was the specific way Woody Allen was using relationships at the time that didn't seem to me to be quite honest.

HETI: How was it not honest?

DIDION: I mean, I saw those movies, and people were talking about relationships in them, and that's all that was happening. It just didn't work for me.

HETI: It was an interesting piece for me to read, because those were the first movies I saw. My father's a huge Woody Allen fan, and to me they seemed like reality, because *Annie Hall* and *Manhattan* were the first times I saw adult life depicted. I must have seen those movies a hundred times in my childhood. So reading your essay was like this light going off, like: Oh, this is just one person's artistic interpretation of life, it's not necessarily—

DIDION: Not necessarily the whole deal.

HETI: Yeah, and not documentary. Do you feel like the culture did go in that direction a lot more, where—

DIDION: Well, it did, after. It became kind of the acceptable way of looking at the world.

HETI: Something more transient about human relations?

DIDION: Yeah.

V. EXTREME OR DOOMED COMMITMENTS

HETI: I want to ask you about the idea of the "extreme or doomed commitment." You have a line in *The White Album* where you say, "I came into adult life equipped with an essentially romantic ethic," believing "that salvation lay in extreme and doomed commitments."

DIDION: Right.

HETI: I wonder if you consider marriage or motherhood, or even writing—

DIDION: I did consider marriage and motherhood extreme and doomed commitments. Not out of any experience of them as such, but it was simply the way I looked at things.

HETI: And having experienced motherhood and marriage, do you still see them as extreme and doomed commitments?

DIDION: No, I don't. I mean, not—I don't. I see them as, well, certainly they were for me a kind of salvation.

HETI: Salvation from what?

DIDION: From a loneliness, an aloneness.

HETI: Because the relationship was so intimate, or just the fact of marriage?

DIDION: Just having another person, answering to another person, was very—it was novel to me, and it turned out to be kind of great.

VI. FINDING NO NARRATIVE

HETI: The fragmentation of *Blue Nights* made me think of your essay "Slouching Towards Bethlehem," in which you talk about the reason that these kids are the way they are is because they don't have—

DIDION: Right.

HETI: —any aunts and uncles—

DIDION: Right.

HETI: And I wonder, as a human and as a writer, if you don't have the same people around you, not just family but also friends, also landmarks in a city that you've lived in for many years—because cities change—does one become more fragmented-feeling, more atomized?

DIDION: Well, I think you do, and then you have to learn to deal with that. I mean, that was part of what I was doing in this book. This book was quite personal. I don't mean it was personal because I talked about things in my life that were personal; I mean it was personal in that I was dealing with my own inability to find the narrative.

HETI: So what does it feel like to come out of a book you've written that doesn't have a narrative?

DIDION: Well, it's not an encouraging attitude, but at this moment, I wanted to flat-out deal with the fact that I did not have, at the moment, an encouraging attitude. [*laughs*]

HETI: Writing something fragmented as opposed to narrative, was it a different kind of thinking?

DIDION: Absolutely it was a different kind of thinking. Because what you're normally doing as a writer is trying to find the narrative. And a lot of the pieces I've written over the past ten years or so have had to do with finding the narrative. This was exactly the opposite. This book proceeds from the idea that the narrative isn't there and it's not going to matter.

HETI: So where is the intensity of the thinking located, then, if not in finding the narrative?

DIDION: Well, in the idea that narrative doesn't matter, I guess.

HETI: Does that feel more true to you than being able to find a narrative? Is that a deeper truth?

DIDION: At the moment it seems so to me, yes. That's kind of what this turned out to be about.

HETI: Do you feel like if you hadn't written the book, that truth would sort of be hovering, but not fully realized in you?

DIDION: Yes. Writing is always a way, for me, of coming to some sort of understanding that I can't reach otherwise.

HETI: How do you think writing works to bring one to an understanding?

DIDION: You mean how does it bring one to an understanding that one can't reach by some other method?

HETI: Yeah.

DIDION: It forces you to think. It forces you to work the thing through. Nothing comes to us out of the blue, very easily, you know. So if you want to understand what you're thinking, you kind of have to work it through and write it. And the only way to work it through, for me, is to write it.

HETI: I guess that has probably been true your whole life.

DIDION: Yeah, it has.

VII. AFTER CHRISTMAS

HETI: In what you're going to write next or what you're writing now, is—

DIDION: I'm not writing now. I wish I were. I haven't written—I have to do something. I'm going to write a couple of pieces next, but I can't seem to focus in on them. In the spring I'm going to try to focus in on something.

HETI: Something assigned to you or something you come up with yourself?

DIDION: Well, eventually you always have to come up with it yourself. It began with something that was suggested to me by an editor, but part of the process will be trying to translate it into something I came up with myself.

HETI: Does it feel different to live when you're not working on something?

DIDION: It feels very different. I don't like it.

HETI: Does it feel kind of like—for me it feels mushy.

DIDION: Mushy, loose in the world, yeah. I can hardly wait to get home. I'm going home tomorrow, on a train, and I have to go to California next week, so I'll be gone again. When I think about when my life will be normal again, it's basically after Christmas.

HETI: So all you're doing is looking forward to After Christmas right now?

DIDION: I am focusing on After Christmas. That's my narrative. [*laughs*]

HETI: And that's when things will settle down, you'll be able to sit at a desk and so on.

DIDION: Sit at a desk, and in the same place every day, yes.

HETI: And that's more vividly living?

DIDION: Yeah.

VIII. FINDING THE RHYTHM

HETI: When do you feel like you're most writing?

DIDION: When I'm finding the rhythm.

HETI: Are there times when you're writing when you feel like you're evading writing?

DIDION: Of course there are times. There must be times when everybody writes when they feel they're evading writing.

HETI: And what is the nature of the evasion? Not thinking?

DIDION: Not thinking, yeah. Not thinking.

IX. A LIFETIME OF MAGICAL LIVING

HETI: You called your previous book *The Year of Magical Thinking,* and in your essay "Sentimental Journeys" you said that New Yorkers, in trying to recover from a highly publicized rape, relied on certain "magical gestures," thinking it could affect their fate. I wonder if you have some sense of what makes us so superstitious? Is it about hope or a lack of control, or why we are such deeply superstitious creatures? We can't even get away from it.

DIDION: No, we can't. Well, I think it's just part of the way we are programmed.

HETI: What does it ultimately give us, do you think?

DIDION: Well, ultimately it gives us a narrative, I guess. There seems to be no way around it. We need one. And it's a sad moment when you can't find one.

HETI: When you look back on your life, is its narrative the narrative you literally wrote yourself?

DIDION: Yes, I would say it was.

X. THE BOTTOM OF THE SEA

HETI: Do you think if you hadn't written, hadn't been a writer, could there have been some completely other—

DIDION: Oh, I wonder. I wanted to be an oceanographer, actually. And when I was out of school and living in New York and working for a magazine, I actually went out to the Scripps Institute, which is now UC San Diego, but then it was just the Scripps Institution of Oceanography, run by the University of California, and I asked them what I would have to do to become an oceanographer. And basically they said I would have to go back to high school, you know. I hadn't taken any of the science courses that would enable me to take the science courses that I would need to take in order to go to . . . any place. So I abandoned the idea of being an oceanographer, but I can see myself still as an oceanographer, if I could get to that point.

HETI: Does it seem like a happier life?

DIDION: A happier life? I don't know. I've liked being a writer.

HETI: It's a different way of going underwater.

DIDION: It's a way of going underwater, yes. Well, I've always been interested in how deep it was, you know.

THE LAST
INTERVIEW

INTERVIEW BY LUCY FELDMAN
TIME
JANUARY 22, 2021

Joan Didion suffers no fools. And nor should she have to. Her résumé is the stuff of legends, from launching her career as a college senior by winning an essay contest sponsored by *Vogue*, which landed her a job at the magazine, to writing one of the first major pieces that cast doubt on the guilt of the since-exonerated Central Park Five. She won a National Book Award and was a finalist for a Pulitzer Prize for a searing book, *The Year of Magical Thinking*, on that most delicate and timeless of subjects—grief—fusing journalistic observation with wrenching personal history. She shopped for Linda Kasabian. She interviewed a five-year-old high on LSD. She starred in a Céline ad as an octogenarian. Dissections of her politics aside, Didion will forever be a certain type of person's idea of a deity—the literary, the cool. She is a chronicler of our world, a writer who dissolves shared delusions to present cold reality with style.

So, when the exceedingly rare opportunity to interview Didion presents itself, one takes it. The writer, now eighty-six and enduring the pandemic from home in New York, is preparing to release her latest essay collection, *Let Me Tell You What I Mean*, coming January 26. The book collects twelve pieces from 1968 to 2000, on topics as varied as Martha Stewart, Gamblers Anonymous, Nancy Reagan and the art of writing. Together, they spotlight moments in Didion's progression as wordsmith and reporter along-side moments in culture. Ahead of the new book's release, Didion indulged *Time* in a few questions.

LUCY FELDMAN: A question that must be asked in these try-ing times: How are you feeling?

JOAN DIDION: I feel fine. Slightly bored, but fine.

FELDMAN: You once said that the bout with vertigo and nausea you had in the summer of 1968 was not an inap-propriate response to that period. What's an appropriate response to 2020?

DIDION: Vertigo and nausea sound right.

FELDMAN: You wrote two of the defining books on grief, *The Year of Magical Thinking* and *Blue Nights*. What would you say to the millions who have lost loved ones in the past year?

DIDION: I don't know. I don't know that there's anything to say.

FELDMAN: Do you fear death?

DIDION: No. Well, yes, of course.

FELDMAN: Do you have hope?

DIDION: Hope for what? Not particularly, no.

FELDMAN: New York has completely changed since the pandemic hit. What do you miss most?

DIDION: I miss having my friends to dinner. On the other hand, my wine bills have gone down.

FELDMAN: Which feels more like home: New York or California?

DIDION: Both.

FELDMAN: What makes a better journalist: the ability to empathize, or the ability to observe with detachment? Which is your greater strength?

DIDION: I don't know that I'm good at either.

FELDMAN: What do you make of the old adage, write what you know?

DIDION: I don't make anything of it.

FELDMAN: Do you ever reread your past writing? If so, what do you think?

DIDION: Sometimes I do. Sometimes I think something is well done, sometimes I think, "Whoops."

FELDMAN: What does it mean to you to be called the voice of your generation?

DIDION: I don't have the slightest idea.

FELDMAN: You famously wrote a piece in 1991 suggesting that the Central Park Five were wrongfully convicted. How did you feel when they were exonerated?

DIDION: However I felt didn't get me or them anywhere.

FELDMAN: How does it feel to be a fashion icon?

DIDION: I don't know that I am one.

FELDMAN: Is there anything you wish to achieve that you have not?

DIDION: Figuring out how to work my television.

FELDMAN: And what would you watch?

DIDION: Aside from the news, nothing comes to mind. Documentaries, maybe. Some series.

FELDMAN: What are you most looking forward to in 2021?

DIDION: An Easter party, if it can be given.

JOAN DIDION is widely considered to be one of the most influential writers of the twentieth century. Born in Sacramento, California, in 1934, she moved to New York City to begin her writing career after receiving a bachelor of arts in English from the University of California, Berkeley, in 1956. She worked as a promotional copywriter and associate feature editor at *Vogue*. It was during her tenure at *Vogue* that she wrote her fist novel, *Run, River*. Writer John Gregory Dunne helped her edit the book, and they married in 1964. They moved to Los Angeles shortly afterward, where they adopted a daughter, Quintana Roo Dunne, in 1966. Didion published her first collection of nonfiction pieces, titled *Slouching Towards Bethlehem*, in 1968, which is considered to be a seminal example of New Journalism. Novels *Play It as It Lays* and *A Book of Common Prayer* followed in 1970 and 1977, respectively. In 1979, she published her second collection of nonfiction, entitled *The White Album*. She began to cowrite screenplays with Dunne in 1971, with *The Panic at Needle Park*. An adaptation of her own novel *Play It as It Lays* followed, along with the script for the 1976 remake of *A Star Is Born*. She continued publishing both novels and books of nonfiction, including *Salvador*, *Democracy*, *Miami*, *After Henry*, and *The Last Thing He Wanted* throughout the 1980s, '90s, and 2000s. In 2003, Dunne died suddenly of a heart attack. She wrote the memoir *The Year of Magical Thinking* covering his death and its aftermath. Her daughter, Quintana Roo, passed away shortly afteward, and Didion wrote another memoir, *Blue Nights*, in 2011 about her relationship with her late daughter. Joan Didion passed away due to complications of Parkinson's disease at home in Manhattan on December 23, 2021, at the age of eighty-seven.

PATRICIA LOCKWOOD is a poet, novelist, and essayist. Her 2021 debut novel, *No One Is Talking About This*, was a finalist for the Booker Prize. Her 2017 memoir, *Priestdaddy*, won the Thurber Prize for American Humor. Her poetry collections include *Motherland Fatherland Homelandsexuals*, a 2014 *New York Times* Notable Book. Since 2019, she has been a contributing editor for *The London Review of Books*.

HILTON ALS is a staff writer and theater critic for *The New Yorker* magazine. His books include *White Girls* and *The Women*. In 2017, he won the Pulitzer Prize for Criticism. He is also a recipient of the Windham-Campbell Literature Prize (nonfiction).

SARA DAVIDSON is a journalist, novelist, and screenwriter. A former reporter at *The Boston Globe*, she has written for *Harper's Magazine*, *Esquire*, *The New York Times*, *Rolling Stone*, and *The Atlantic Monthly* among others, and is the author of the bestselling group biography *Loose Change*.

SALLY DAVIS was a producer at Pacifica Radio.

DAVE EGGERS is a writer, editor, and publisher. He is the founder of *Timothy McSweeney's Quarterly Concern* and the author of many books, including *A Heartbreaking Work of Staggering Genius*, *What Is the What*, and, most recently, *The Every*. He is the recipient of many literary prizes and honors, including an honorary doctorate of letters from Brown University, the Dayton Literary Peace Prize, and the PEN Center USA's Award of Honor. He has been a finalist for the Pulitzer Prize, the National Book Award, the California Book Awards, and the National Book Critics Circle Award. In 2005, he was named one of *Time*'s 100 Most Influential People.

LUCY FELDMAN is a senior editor for *Time*, where she leads the magazine's coverage of books and authors. She has held roles at *Vanity Fair* and the *Wall Street Journal*, where she ran the WSJ Book Club.

TERRY GROSS is the producer and host of *Fresh Air*. She assumed the role in 1975, when it was still a local program. *Fresh Air* won a Peabody Award in 1993 for its "probing questions, revelatory interviews, and unusual insights." In 2003, Gross received public radio's highest honor, the Edward R. Murrow Award. She is the author of *All I Did Was Ask: Conversations with Writers, Actors, Musicians, and Artists*.

SHEILA HETI was the former interviews editor at *The Believer*. She is the author of several books, including *How Should a Person Be?*, *Motherhood*, and, most recently, *Pure Colour*.

HARI KUNZRU is the author of several novels, including *White Tears*, *Red Pill*, and the *New York Times* Notable Book of the Year *Transmission*. In 2014, he was awarded a John Simon Guggenheim Fellowship, and in 2016 he became a fellow at the American Academy in Berlin.

MARTIN TORGOFF is an American journalist, author, documentary filmmaker, and director and producer of television, who has worked extensively in the fields of music and American popular culture. He is best known for his book *Can't Find My Way Home: America in the Great Stoned Age, 1945–2000*, a narrative cultural history of illicit drugs.

THE LAST INTERVIEW SERIES

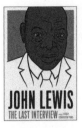

JOHN LEWIS:
THE LAST INTERVIEW

$16.99 / $22.99 CAN

978-1-61219-962-7
ebook: 978-1-61219-963-4

FRIDA KAHLO:
THE LAST INTERVIEW

$16.99 / $22.99 CAN

978-1-61219-875-0
ebook: 978-1-61219-876-7

FRED ROGERS:
THE LAST INTERVIEW

$16.99 / $21.99 CAN

978-1-61219-895-8
ebook: 978-1-61219-896-5

TONI MORRISON:
THE LAST INTERVIEW

$16.99 / $22.99 CAN

978-1-61219-873-6
ebook: 978-1-61219-874-3

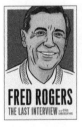

SHIRLEY CHISHOLM:
THE LAST INTERVIEW

$16.99 / $22.99 CAN

978-1-61219-897-2
ebook: 978-1-61219-898-9

GRAHAM GREENE:
THE LAST INTERVIEW

$16.99 / $22.99 CAN

978-1-61219-814-9
ebook: 978-1-61219-815-6

RUTH BADER GINSBURG:
THE LAST INTERVIEW

$17.99 / $23.99 CAN

978-1-61219-919-1
ebook: 978-1-61219-920-7

URSULA K. LE GUIN:
THE LAST INTERVIEW

$16.99 / $21.99 CAN

978-1-61219-779-1
ebook: 978-1-61219-780-7

THE LAST INTERVIEW SERIES

**JULIA CHILD:
THE LAST INTERVIEW**

$16.99 / $22.99 CAN

978-1-61219-733-3
ebook: 978-1-61219-734-0

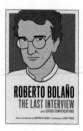

**ROBERTO BOLAÑO:
THE LAST INTERVIEW**

$15.95 / $17.95 CAN

978-1-61219-095-2
ebook: 978-1-61219-033-4

**KURT VONNEGUT:
THE LAST INTERVIEW**

$15.95 / $17.95 CAN

978-1-61219-090-7
ebook: 978-1-61219-091-4

**RAY BRADBURY:
THE LAST INTERVIEW**

$15.95 / $15.95 CAN

978-1-61219-421-9
ebook: 978-1-61219-422-6

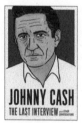

**JOHNNY CASH:
THE LAST INTERVIEW**

$16.99 / $22.99 CAN

978-1-61219-893-4
ebook: 978-1-61219-894-1

**JAMES BALDWIN:
THE LAST INTERVIEW**

$16.99 / $22.99 CAN

978-1-61219-400-4
ebook: 978-1-61219-401-1

**MARILYN MONROE:
THE LAST INTERVIEW**

$16.99 / $22.99 CAN

978-1-61219-877-4
ebook: 978-1-61219-878-1

**GABRIEL GARCÍA
MÁRQUEZ: THE LAST
INTERVIEW**

$15.95 / $15.95 CAN

978-1-61219-480-6
ebook: 978-1-61219-481-3

THE LAST INTERVIEW SERIES

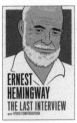

**ERNEST HEMINGWAY:
THE LAST INTERVIEW**

$15.95 / $20.95 CAN

978-1-61219-522-3
ebook: 978-1-61219-523-0

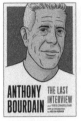

**ANTHONY BOURDAIN:
THE LAST INTERVIEW**

$17.99 / $23.99 CAN

978-1-61219-824-8
ebook: 978-1-61219-825-5

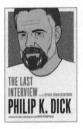

**PHILIP K. DICK:
THE LAST INTERVIEW**

$15.95 / $20.95 CAN

978-1-61219-526-1
ebook: 978-1-61219-527-8

**MARTIN LUTHER KING, JR.:
THE LAST INTERVIEW**

$15.99 / $21.99 CAN

978-1-61219-616-9
ebook: 978-1-61219-617-6

**NORA EPHRON:
THE LAST INTERVIEW**

$15.95 / $20.95 CAN

978-1-61219-524-7
ebook: 978-1-61219-525-4

**CHRISTOPHER HITCHENS:
THE LAST INTERVIEW**

$15.99 / $20.99 CAN

978-1-61219-672-5
ebook: 978-1-61219-673-2

**DAVID BOWIE:
THE LAST INTERVIEW**

$16.99 / $22.99 CAN

978-1-61219-575-9
ebook: 978-1-61219-576-6

**HUNTER S. THOMPSON:
THE LAST INTERVIEW**

$15.99 / $20.99 CAN

978-1-61219-693-0
ebook: 978-1-61219-694-7

THE LAST INTERVIEW SERIES

**BILLIE HOLIDAY:
THE LAST INTERVIEW**

$16.99 / $22.99 CAN

978-1-61219-674-9
ebook: 978-1-61219-675-6

**KATHY ACKER:
THE LAST INTERVIEW**

$16.99 / $21.99 CAN

978-1-61219-731-9
ebook: 978-1-61219-732-6

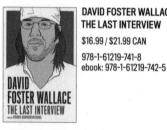

**DAVID FOSTER WALLACE:
THE LAST INTERVIEW**

$16.99 / $21.99 CAN

978-1-61219-741-8
ebook: 978-1-61219-742-5

**JORGE LUIS BORGES:
THE LAST INTERVIEW**

$15.95 / $15.95 CAN

978-1-61219-204-8
ebook: 978-1-61219-205-5

**PRINCE:
THE LAST INTERVIEW**

$16.99 / $22.99 CAN

978-1-61219-745-6
ebook: 978-1-61219-746-3

**HANNAH ARENDT:
THE LAST INTERVIEW**

$15.95 / $15.95 CAN

978-1-61219-311-3
ebook: 978-1-61219-312-0

**JANE JACOBS:
THE LAST INTERVIEW**

$15.95 / $20.95 CAN

978-1-61219-534-6
ebook: 978-1-61219-535-3

**LOU REED:
THE LAST INTERVIEW**

$15.95 / $15.95 CAN

978-1-61219-478-3
ebook: 978-1-61219-479-0